Black Students' Perceptions

Studies in the
Postmodern Theory of Education

Joe L. Kincheloe and Shirley R. Steinberg
General Editors

Vol. 199

PETER LANG
New York • Washington, D.C./Baltimore • Bern
Frankfurt am Main • Berlin • Brussels • Vienna • Oxford

R. Deborah Davis

Black Students' Perceptions

The Complexity of Persistence to Graduation at an American University

PETER LANG
New York • Washington, D.C./Baltimore • Bern
Frankfurt am Main • Berlin • Brussels • Vienna • Oxford

Library of Congress Cataloging-in-Publication Data

Davis, R. Deborah.
Black students' perceptions: the complexity of persistence to
graduation at an American university / R. Deborah Davis.
p. cm. — (Counterpoints; vol. 199)
Includes bibliographical references (p.) and index.
1. African Americans—Education (Higher)—New York (State)—
Syracuse—Longitudinal studies. 2. College environment—New York
(State)—Syracuse—Longitudinal studies. 3. Syracuse University—
Longitudinal studies. I. Title. II. Counterpoints (New York, N.Y.); v. 199.
LC2781.7 .D38   378.747'66—dc21   2002016253
ISBN 0-8204-5539-3
ISSN 1058-1634

Bibliographic information published by **Die Deutsche Bibliothek**.
Die Deutsche Bibliothek lists this publication in the "Deutsche
Nationalbibliografie"; detailed bibliographic data is available
on the Internet at http://dnb.ddb.de/.

Cover design by Sophie Boorsch Appel

The paper in this book meets the guidelines for permanence and durability
of the Committee on Production Guidelines for Book Longevity
of the Council of Library Resources.

© 2004 Peter Lang Publishing, Inc., New York
275 Seventh Avenue, 28th Floor, New York, NY 10001
www.peterlangusa.com

All rights reserved.
Reprint or reproduction, even partially, in all forms such as microfilm,
xerography, microfiche, microcard, and offset strictly prohibited.

Printed in the United States of America

This book is dedicated to the memory of my mother,
Naomi Powell Lewis, and my friend, Willie J. Hill.

❦ Table of Contents

List of Figures and Tables ix

Acknowledgments xi

1. Introduction 1

2. Social Context in the Early 1990s 19

3. Student Development/Black Student Development 29

4. The Campus As the Black Students See It 47

5. Students' Perceptions of Race 73

6. Talk About Being Visible and Invisible 87

7. A Different Perception of the Black Students' Experience 109

8. Interpretations 121

References 137

Index 147

⚜ Figures

Figure 1.1 Syracuse University Black Enrollment 10

Figure 1.2 Where Black Students Sent Their SAT Scores 11

Figure 3.1 Chickering's Seven Vectors 34

Figure 3.2 Perry's Model of Intellectual and Ethical Development 36

Figure 3.3 A Conception of Adolescent to Adult Development (A Juxtaposition) 38

Figure 3.4 Cross's Stages of Black Identity 39

Figure 3.5 Shadows of the Black College Student Experience 41

Figure 3.6 The Black Students' College Experience at a Predominantly White Institution.. 44

Figure 7 The Black Students' College Experience at a Predominantly White Institution...................................... 114

⚜ Tables

Table 2.1 Black Undergraduate Enrollment 1980–1990 20

Table 2.2 Four-Year Graduation Figures 20

ॐ Acknowledgments

First and foremost I thank God for the strength and blessings to persist, even when I got in my own way. I extend my thanks to my children—Melanie, Charlese, Marvin, and Tammy, and my grandchildren—Rhyan, Brandon, Jordan, Krystal, and Myles—for the time they gave me to do this work. My deepest appreciation goes out to the student participants whose lived experiences provide the character for this text. To them I am forever grateful.

Special thanks to my sister, Yvonne, to Pat Tinto and Joan Burstyn who opened the path that I might make my way through. To my Sistahs group, I say thank you for your spiritual and emotional support, and unity.

I would also like to thank my editor, Heidi Burns, for her patience through my illness and thoughtful comments regarding my text. I am very grateful.

A special gratitude to Paula K. Kazmark and Andrea Mujahid Moore for the listening ear and the midnight oil. The list of persons who have touched my life or who have allowed me a space in theirs during this process is much too long to cite here, but please know that God knows you were there.

I would also like to thank the following for their permission to reprint the following work:

A Perception..., from "What Is a Feminist?" by Angela Williams, ©1995, an unpublished manuscript.

"Talking race on campus: Reported speech sequences of racism and interracial contact on a university campus." Paper presented at the Georgetown University Conference, Advances in Discourse Analysis, Washington, D.C. ©1995. by Richard Buttny, Ph.D., Syracuse University.

❋ Introduction

Black students are achieving at a lower rate and graduating at a much lower percentage rate than white students at predominantly white institutions. This is the case even at institutions featuring supportive services and staffs specifically designated for the student who is educationally and economically disadvantaged. The widely held stereotype that the majority of students with "educational and economic disadvantages" are Black and poor seems to dictate the actions of White students, faculty, and staff as they relate to Black students. Stereotypes—originating during the time of slavery and currently supported in the mainstream media of Blacks as being violent, lazy, and shiftless, criminal types posing a threatening image to society—have made their way onto college campuses. Students candidly talked about the disparity in treatment they believed was based on them being viewed in this stereotypical manner. Black students continue to be treated as if they need to be remediated to meet standards historically set by White educators. Just look at the continued commitment of resources to programs for "disadvantaged" minority students (Armstrong-West & de la Teja, 1988).

The gap is widening between who enters and who graduates from our institutions of higher education and dropout rates are increasing. I wanted to hear the students' side of the story. This book presents the Black experience of a cohort of students over a five-year period. Students' comments give a different perspective to the discourse on why some Black students persist when so many choose the alternate path. Many new questions are generated to refocus institutional retention strategies.

Since the early 1960s and the onset of the Civil Rights Movement, counselors, teachers, administrators, and scholars have been looking at the phenomenon of Black and minority students on predominantly White college and university campuses and how the college experience affects academic achievement (Cope & Hanna, 1975; Astin, 1977, 1982; Allen, 1984; Fleming, 1984; Nettles et al., 1985; Mow & Nettles, 1990; Pascarella & Terenzini, 1991). The terms *Black*, *White*, and *Biracial* will be capitalized throughout this text as the significant characteristic in this discussion of the experiences of students identified in racial terms, designated by the color of their skin. Instances where the words *Black*, *White*, and *Biracial* are found in quotations, represent those terms as they have been written in their respective original copy.

The purpose of this study was to learn from the perceptions of Black/African American students about their experiences on a predominantly White university campus, including what it meant to them to have a precollege experience and how they found comfortable spaces in what the students termed a "hostile environment." From the students' responses to open-ended questions, I looked at the negative and positive experiences most often shared and pondered: *Why* do these experiences occur for Black/African American students? *How* do these experiences differ from or how similar are they to the experiences of White students on a predominantly White campus? This book grew out of my general concern as an African American, for the fact that, although there has been a steady increase in the numbers of Black students, there has been a steady decline in the percentage of growth, albeit an increase in the proportion of Black students graduating from institutions of higher education.

It is my assumption here that the *social climate* is something that occurs as interaction between and among students, faculty, and staff, takes place in the campus environment. Conversely, the *academic environment* is a setting or atmosphere, conducive to learning, which is presumably structured by university policy and philosophy. Generally, the tenets of the campus atmosphere are written and distributed in the institution's literature such as the catalog or student and employee handbooks. Everyone plays a part in creating the actual climate and environment that exists on a campus. Students' responses enable us to learn what makes a positive, supportive, and comfortable climate for them as opposed to what they found to be negative, painful, and disruptive to their academic success.

Because of its proximity to New York City, Syracuse University has an Admissions Office, The Lubin House, located in Manhattan for the purpose of recruitment and alumni relations. Syracuse University boasts successful recruitment efforts among the Black and Hispanic populations located in the five boroughs of New York: Bronx, Brooklyn, Manhattan, Long Island, and Queens. Predominantly Black/Hispanic high schools are the primary feeder schools for students from groups underrepresented on Syracuse University's campus. My data indicate that students feel that being "from the City" has significance for their experience on this campus.

The Black students recruited from New York, the New England states, New Jersey, and Pennsylvania come from home environments which could be representative of all socioeconomic levels: lower class, middle class, upper middle class, and even wealthy with many of mixed heritage being descendants of second-generation immigrants from the West Indies, British Isles, and Africa, and of migrants from the southern United States. Obviously, the university does not depend solely on the Northeast for its Black enrollment. Owing to a national sports reputation, exemplary schools and colleges, and world renowned faculty and programs, Syracuse University attracts Black students from areas urban, suburban, and rural across the United States and from many other countries.

Regardless of their geographic roots, there are many terms used to *describe* and *categorize* nonwhite students of African descent in the literature on education. I need to clarify terms used in this text. Descriptors include: Black, of the African diaspora, African American, Biracial, people of color, minorities, and other minorities. *Black* is the term I use when talking about the heterogeneous group of students of the African diaspora whose skin is any of the many shades from light brown to rich black in color. Black also includes, but is not limited to, people who are African American, Caribbean born, European born of Black parents, and Biracial persons with African heritage. In this study, *of the African diaspora* is used to indicate Black students whose origins are not specifically known but who are of African descent (American or not) and who include themselves in the community of Black students. *African American* indicates those Black students born in any of the fifty states of the United States of America. *Biracial* is the term I use for those students with Black/White racial heritage. *People of color* is a term used here to indicate nonwhite students of various ethnic and national backgrounds previously considered, by society, within the larger term *minorities*. The term *other minorities* is used when referring to students or scholars from other than Black ethnic or cultural groups. The term *European American* will be used interchangeably with White to designate students of the predominant group on campus.

In American education and sociology/social science research there are many terms that have come to be known as descriptors of African American culture and people, particularly students at all levels. Terms often change over time or the interpretation of them is changed to fit the particular time or context. Look at the retention literature and many of the terms we have come to accept as understood by all to mean "minorities," particularly African Americans: *underprepared, underrepresented, at risk, high risk* (each term with its own duality) just to list the most obvious. Then, there is the interdisciplinary literature (i.e., psychology, social work, child and family studies) reflecting the growth and development of our perceptions of students from other than majority groups.

None of the above labels are used either by me or my respondents to explain our identity. These terms will be used only as they appear in original citations. Upon investigation, I found there were multiple meanings given for all of these terms, most depending on the particular circumstance being considered. My focus is on the *students' perceptions* of their experiences. Some of the more problematic—in terms of the all-encompassing nature in which they are used—are the reference group names African American and Black, Hispanic, and Latino, as well as American Indian, Native American, Aleutian Native, and Indigenous People. The connotations of these terms have been affected by stereotypes that have been promulgated by the scientific and academic communities and the mainstream popular media. Group terms are used and abused as all-inclusive. The category *African American* is used by institutions as a catch-all phrase for persons of color who do not have distinctive *international* features or language. As is the case in the larger society, however, the African American student comes from all different social, economic backgrounds and ethnic combinations. Black students also come in all different shades of brown from the very light "passing for White" color of mixed lineage, to the rich dark black of full African descent.

Several researchers (Astin, 1990; Bean, 1990; Nettles, 1991; H. H. Smith, 1991; Tinto, 1994) have provided data concerning the extent to which Black and minority students have been successful at negotiating the transition to college. Specifically, Alexander Astin (1982), Mow & Nettles (1990), and Michael Nettles (1991), senior scholars in the study of student retention, identified elements critical to persistence in academic studies. Since the early seventies, scholars (Gibbs, 1973; Gibson & Ogbu, 1991) have discussed motivational factors related to the historical background and learning styles of African American students in the predominantly White educational system in America. Few studies have focused on the experience of Black students past the freshman year or on the perceptions of the students themselves.

The purpose of this study was to ask the students what they thought about their experiences on a campus where the majority of the students were not like them in terms of race and social location. Four overarching questions have driven this inquiry:

1. How do African American students perceive their college experiences at Syracuse University?

2. What is the importance of the Summer Institute pre-freshman program in the persistence decision, as perceived by the African American student?
3. What are some of the reasons, as perceived by the students, why African American students persist in predominately White institutions in relation to social integration and their commitment to graduation?
4. What common themes among the students' experiences have implications for the development of interventions to increase their graduation rate?

Before beginning my academic studies, I had an opportunity to work with student leaders, provide a service in the university, and observe their development as student leaders over a period of approximately two years. This was during 1988 and 1989, including summers. I noticed a decided difference in the demeanor, and frustration, between the Black and Hispanic students and the White students during this time period. What caused this difference?

Between 1987 and 1989, there was widespread racial tension on the campuses of America. At Syracuse University, Black students joined the protest over the tuition increase, which they said "hit African American students the hardest." A steady stream of "racially motivated incidents" was reported, and there was constant discussion about racism in the Opinion section of *The Daily Orange* student newspaper. According to newspaper accounts, there was an increased amount of student activism among the African American students in response to administrative in-action regarding the African American Studies (AAS) department. In 1991, I decided to investigate the students' perceptions of their experiences since their freshman year on a predominantly White campus. This book describes this study, which I began in October 1991.

Figures in the 1990 summary of the *Chronicle of Higher Education* (1992) indicate that over 1,223,000 Black undergraduates are enrolled in predominantly White institutions (August 26, 1992). It has been estimated that more than one million (80%) Black college youths are choosing to attend predominantly White institutions instead of historically Black colleges and universities (HBCUs) (Mow & Nettles, 1990; Deskins, 1991; Allen et al., 1991). In some cases where Black students have been asked their perceptions of their experience, it has been in sharp contrast to that of the establishment (Willie & McCord, 1972; Adler & Adler, 1991). Such misperception can potentially inhibit the success of Black students at predominantly White institutions. Walter Allen et al, in *Colleges in Black and White*, assert that "Black and minority students [have] been the subject of very little systematic, quantitative, and analytic research" (1991, p. 2). Institutions have fallen short because they do not understand the Black students' cultural background and have not been committed to a longitudinal research approach.

This study was conducted at one medium-sized, private, research university in the eastern United States. Syracuse University was chosen for three major reasons: its consistent percentage of Black and minority students (10%+); its historically active Black student organizations and its archives; and the university's commitment to the Black and Latino Alumni Association. It is not the intent that the findings from this study be generalized to all predominantly White institutions or to all Black students. The information presented here is best understood as the perceptions of students on one university campus who are obviously different by skin color and racial/cultural and ethnic definition from the majority of the students there.

Syracuse University (SU) has over an eighty-year history of educating Black students according to Robert Hill, Vice President, University Relations. In an article "Black leadership, a tradition at SU" (*Syracuse Herald American*, 1986), Hill wrote of "Everett Browning Williams leading the Syracuse University [academic] debate team to victory over Yale" in 1917. Hill continued to chronicle the "tradition of Black leadership" that has been the legacy of SU. Hill presented this list, dates, and accomplishments:

- Conrad Lynn '32—civil rights attorney-activist

- Gladys Bryant '29—first Black woman to graduate from SU—grandniece of the great underground railroad conductor Harriet Tubman—not allowed lodging on campus, she lived off-campus with Negro families
- Ellsworth Hasbrouck—one of Chicago's most distinguished surgeons
- Wilmeth Sidat-Singh—football player; one of the Tuskegee Flyers who "lost his life in the air force experimental program to determine if Blacks could learn to fly in combat."
- Horace Morris—one-time head of the United Way & Greater New York Fund in New York City, [who during] 1945—experienced being the only Black on the football team at SU.
- John Williams '50—author and professor at Rutgers; established a chapter of Alpha Phi Alpha, the national Black fraternity founded at Cornell a generation earlier.
- Avatus Stone—reigning football hero, president of a successful consulting firm
- John Devereau—'56-'57 became president of the men students on campus
- Vincent Cohen '57—first Black basketball hero at SU—"Washington attorney, formidable litigator, and reported to be the highest paid Black lawyer in America."
- Jim Brown '57—football legend, also excelled at track and basketball—now actor, producer, and social activist
- John Brown '61—bank president in Pittsburgh
- Billy Hunter '65—was in the Carter administration as U.S. attorney for northern California
- Floyd Little '67—National Football Hall of Famer for the Denver Broncos—president of a TV station and a car dealership in California
- John Mackey '63—a leader in formation of NFL Players Association—a businessman in California
- Dave Bing '66—an SU economics major—star with Detroit Pistons—became president of a Detroit steel company and

won Minority Small Businessman of the Year Award from President Reagan.

Although the accomplishments are highly commendable, we cannot help but notice that the majority of these professionals were athletes during their stay at the university. Much has changed but much remains the same—Blacks are still disproportionately recruited to play sports on today's campuses. In the cohort I interviewed, a few students indicated that the national sports reputation of Syracuse University was one of the key factors in their decision to come to the university, although none of the participants were athletes.

The Black graduates of Syracuse University exemplified the "Talented Tenth" that W. E. B. DuBois spoke about in his memorial address originally printed in *Boule Journal* in 1948 (cited in Lewis, 1995, p. 347). DuBois explained the term as "meaning leadership of the Negro race in America by a trained few." Black students in my study also considered that they had "made it" to have been *accepted* by Syracuse University. Impressive is Hill's list of Black graduates prior to the Civil Rights legislation. Blacks were educated at Syracuse by more than just the academic content. The content of their character was strengthened as they learned the skills to get along in the educated White world.

Hill (1986) notes: "They did not feel disadvantaged, deprived, detested or despised. They knew they were Black on a predominantly White campus. That settled, they got on with their business to great effect" (p. E-4). Hill further comments that after the Civil Rights Movement "White academia, in an admirable display of will to overcome past exclusions, opened its doors to Black America" (p. E-4). The resulting programs and financial aid allowed the national "ranks of Black college students to soar from approximately .... million, before 1969, to .... 1.1 million by 1982" (Hill, 1986, p. E-4). It was 1969, when Syracuse University became a beneficiary of the first appropriated funds of the State of New York for "independent colleges and universities. . . .. This initiative was entitled the Higher Education Opportunity Program or HEOP." As a result Black student recruitment and enrollment increased (H. Smith, 1991).

According to Hill, in 1986 the combined minority enrollment (African American, Hispanic, Native American, and Asian) at Syracuse, stood at 10 % of all students. This increase, according to Hill, was due primarily to New York State–funded HEOP, which provided financial aid and academic support for disadvantaged students. Recruitment trends at the time drew a large number of students....diverse backgrounds from the New York City area, a proportion consistent with demographic trends in the community served by Syracuse University. Society at large, however, tends to assume that Black students are the primary beneficiaries when attending predominantly White institutions.

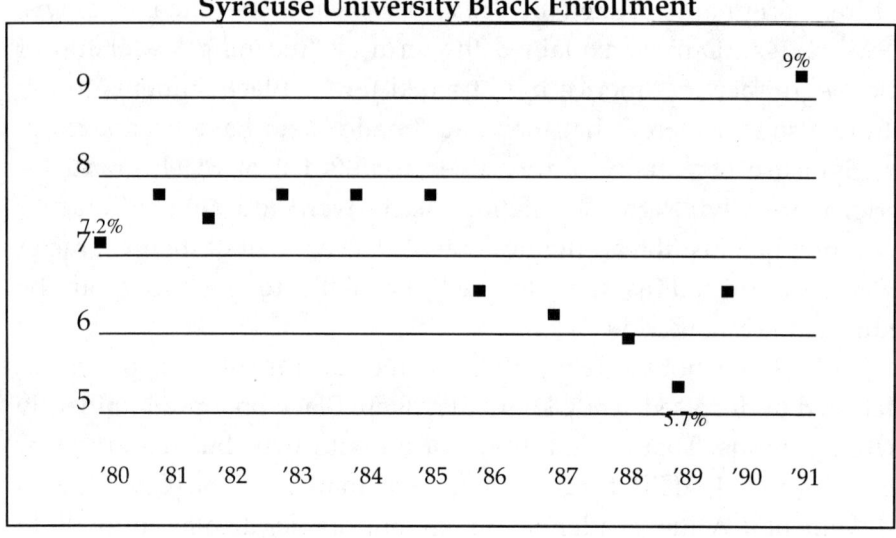

Figure 1.1

Black enrollment at Syracuse University dipped in the mid 1980's. It rose dramatically between 1989 and 1991. The enrollment figures are based on fall enrollment of the year listed. *Source: Syracuse University, March 10, 1992, Herald-Journal, p. A-1*

However, the institution benefits financially and culturally when Black students attend and are active in campus life. At Syracuse

University, the 1980 Black enrollment was at 7.2% (Figure 1.1); by the late 1980s, when total university enrollment increased, the proportion of Blacks declined. In 1989, the proportion of Blacks to total student enrollment was the lowest in the decade (see Figure 1.1).

Where Black Students Sent Their SAT Scores		
School	Scores sent	% + -
1. Howard Univ (DC)	12,161	-5.3 %
2. Hampton Univ (VA	10,637	-0.4
3. Spellman College (GA)	7,588	+4.0
4. Florida A&M Univ	6,103	+8.3
5. No. Carol. A&T State Univ.	6,020	+8.4
6. Clark Atlanta Univ (GA)	5,380	+27.5
7. Morgan state Univ (MD)	4,943	+16.1
8. Virginia State Univ.	4,921	+6.7
9. Florida State Univ.	4,563	+6.4
10. Morehouse College (GA)	4,398	+8.7
11. North Carol. Central Univ.	4,398	+2.7
12. North Carolina State Univ.	4,344	-3.7
13. Syracuse Univ.	4,268	+4.4
14. Norfolk State Univ. (VA)	3,965	NA
15. Univ. of Virginia	3,781	NA
16. New York City Univ.	3,779	NA
17. Univ, of North Carolina	3,737	+2.2
18. Tuskegee Univ. (AL)	3,731	NA
19. South Carolina State Univ.	3,480	NA
20. Georgetown Univ. (DC)	3,426	NA

Figure 1.2

In 1991, 96,738 Black students sent their Scholastic Aptitude Test scores to more than 4,000 colleges and universities throughout the country. Syracuse University was the 13th most popular school. Of predominantly White institutions only Florida State University and North Carolina State University received more test reports. The percentage change is 1990. Source: The College Board. (*Syracuse Herald-Journal*, March 10, 1992)

In 1990 the proportion had begun to turn upward again, though it was still below 7%. Using the blueprint from the American Council on Education, *Minorities on Campus* (1989), institutions looked with renewed interest at retention strategies and their effectiveness. Syracuse University was no exception.

Black student enrollment increased significantly. By 1992, a "9 percent or 1,035 of SU's 11,495 undergraduates were Black." (*Syracuse Herald-Journal*, March 10, 1992, p. A-1). According to 1991 College Board figures, of 4000 institutions nationwide who received Scholastic Aptitude Test scores submitted by Black high school seniors, Syracuse University was the third most popular predominantly White institution overall and the most popular in the Northeast (Figure 1.2). However, retention rates were not keeping up with reported enrollment figures.

The Campus

Syracuse University is an independent, comprehensive research and teaching university located on the east side of a city of approximately 163,860 people (H. Smith, 1991; Syracuse Chamber of Commerce, 1993). Two major highways separate the university and the residents of the Black community nearby from the greater metropolitan area. The university is relatively self-contained with all of the services a student would need within its main, north and south campuses. These are within a radius of approximately 1.5 miles. A major student center, Schine Student Center, was built in 1985 to provide students with a variety of services. This center includes a dining hall, meeting rooms, a game room, TV and study area, quiet study areas, a computer cluster, bookstore, placement center and administrative offices. Schine Student Center is located on the main campus and boasts office space for 26 student organizations; a very large multipurpose auditorium/banquet hall; and a smaller, technically versatile theater room.

Until 1998, this center housed two student-run businesses: an electronics/music/florist/travel services/video and appliance rental store and then a printing and duplicating service that also provided both off-campus housing and student health insurance services. Subsequently, the latter business was dissolved and a new service office—the Office of Multicultural Affairs—was instituted in that space on the lower level.

A major hotel and a parking lot are located across the street from the main campus, as well as a two-block commercial district. Shops, many ethnic restaurants, a florist, a bookstore, a copy center, and bars compete with the university-owned businesses for the students' patronage. There is also a mall that offers health services (dentists, optometrists, and a pharmacy), a post office, and several fast-food restaurants. Students have outlets for many social activities, e.g., dancing, recreational sports, game room (pool, ping pong, and video games). On the north campus and several blocks away are the Continuing Education Division and evening college, the Drama Department, and the performing arts Experimental Theaters.

A second student center was built in 1990, on the south campus "to complement Schine." Goldstein Student Center provides dining and other services to graduate students, with and without families, and undergraduate students who live in "South Campus Housing." It includes a dining hall, meeting rooms, a game room, TV, and quiet study areas, a store run by the bookstore, and administrative offices. This center also contains a laundromat and a nautilus center for easier student access and closer proximity for south campus residents.

There are 40 Greek letter organizations (25 fraternities and 15 sororities), most of which have houses located on the main campus. Chartered, these groups are affiliated with the national Pan-Hellenic and Black Pan-Hellenic Councils. Of these, there are seven Black organizations (4 sororities, 3 fraternities), none of which have houses for their chapters; there was one university-owned house provided for the use of the seven Black Pan-Hellenic groups. The university provides an official liaison to work with all Greek chapters. In addition there were more than 150 other student groups for students to get involved. "At the forefront of these organizations is the Student Government Association (SGA)" (*Syracuse University Student Handbook*, 1991–1992, p. 92). These organizations provided social and academic outlets, as well as opportunities for ethnic, cultural, national, religious, and political affiliation. The benefit of social support—relationships with family, kin, friends, co-workers, acquaintances, and the larger community—among humans has been well documented in sociological literature, although not as conclusively relating to students on college campuses. Fleming (1984) provided a comparative picture of the intellectual development of Black students in Black and White colleges (Davis, 1991).

In 1989, Student Government Association was the overall umbrella organization that managed the monies from the student activity fee each undergraduate student paid to the university. Through a system of parliamentary procedures, funds were allocated to each student group for their programming needs. Just as SGA was the umbrella for all campus groups, the Student African American Society (S.A.S.) was the umbrella for the African American groups. They functioned similarly for the Black-student constituents except that SGA was open to all students as the advocacy group regarding university proceedings; S.A.S. served as the political advocacy group in regard to constituent issues and programming for Black/African American students.

Under the S.A.S. umbrella, there were several preprofessional groups who encouraged Black students in their career development. Examples of the more active were: Minority Pre-health, Pre-professional Management, National Society of Black Engineers (NSBE), National Association for the Advancement of Colored People (NAACP), and the National Association of Negro Business and Professional Women's Clubs (NANBPWC). All groups' funds were allocated from the SGA Senate Budget. S.A.S., from its portion of the budget, offered sponsorship of speakers, events, and collaboration on programming ideas of the more focused constituent groups.

Syracuse University, like the majority of higher education institutions, is concerned about enrollment and retention. In 1988–1989, enrollment included 12,401 undergraduates, 3,707 graduate students, and 713 law students (Syracuse University *FACTS*, 1988–89). Approximately 20% percent of the students were minorities; of these

20%, one-half were African Americans. Counted as "other minorities" were Hispanic, Native American, Pacific Islanders, and Asian American students.

From the mid-1980s, Syracuse University experienced a decline in the proportion of African American enrollment, as well as experiencing no growth in the number of faculty in the African American Studies (AAS) Department. According to a *Post Standard* article entitled "Minority Professors Still a Rarity at SU," "The department has been without a permanent chairman for more than a year. Also, no new faculty positions have been added since Afro-American Studies became a department in the College of Arts and Sciences 11 years ago" (Nelis, *Syracuse Post Standard*, February 6, 1989, p. 7).

In 1986 the university made a commitment to hire at least 26 minority faculty members over a period of two years. Despite the university's push toward acquiring 26 minority professors, the number was 21 in February 1989, which indicated that only 2.2 of the 944 full-time faculty was made up minorities. Students in this study talked about the value of having Black faculty and administrators as role models, because they were living proof that in fact Blacks can achieve in academic settings. Similar statements were made about Black role models seen in the corporate world while students were serving at internships. The presence of Black role models was motivating, their absence discouraging.

Whereas university administrators said they were committed to hiring a larger number of minority faculty, they claimed the pool of qualified minority candidates was too small. Consequently, there had been no permanent chairperson for the AAS Department since 1982 (*Daily Orange*, September 11, 1989). According to the student newspaper, the *Daily Orange*, in a front-page article published in 1989:

> Last year, faculty members and students, particularly members of the Student African American Society, voiced dissatisfaction with SU's efforts to improve the department. SAS protests last year included a demonstration February 27 when 120 SAS members confronted Chancellor Melvin A. Eggers at the Chancellor's Roundtable meeting of student leaders. The

group's efforts, led by SAS President Quentin Stith, culminated in an April protest of about 400 students at the dedication ceremony of the Science and Technology Center and later at a luncheon in Goldstein Auditorium. (1989, pp. A-1, A-4)

Black students acted in a unified effort to force the university to recognize its responsibility both to hire a chairperson and to increase the staff in the AAS Department as a means to provide not only Black students but *all* students on campus with the opportunity to learn about African American history and culture.

Subsequently, a new chairperson for the AAS Department was hired in the fall of 1990. This chairperson espoused the philosophy of a "university" being an institution of only one race—the human race. His philosophy was expressed in his classes and broadly voiced in public forums. He admonished the university as a collective—administration, faculty, and students—on the futility of continuing the use of racial designations, Black and White, and such terms as *foreign, minority, and majority* (Hare, 1991). Student interviews and published documents at that time attest to how the influence of the AAS Department and the circumstances surrounding the selection of the chair had a great deal to do with the students' perceptions of the university. Key personalities such as the AAS chair, the presidents of the S.A.S. student group, as well as prominent national speakers embodied a confidence and affirmation of a Black identity. An evolving sense of Black identity was expressed in a collective struggle. Students of color eschewed reference to themselves as a collective group called "minorities." Instead, they emerged as African Americans, Caribbean Americans, Latino/as, and Biracial individuals. Of course this confidence and pride was, in some respects, misunderstood, as evidenced by an increase in charges, by Whites, of separatism and exclusion, and by Blacks, of racism, harassment, ignorance, and insensitivity.

During 1988 and 1989, students rallied around issues important to African American students on campus. In the *Daily Orange*, there were lead articles, op-ed opinion pieces, and letters to the editor. Ongoing discussion chronicled the escalating activism around what the Black students perceived as institutional racism. According to accounts in both prominent university newspapers—the *Daily Orange* student newspaper and *The Record*, the official campus newspaper—the campus was fraught with a high level of institutional racism, whether deliberate or not. During this period there were more charges and counter charges made in letters to the editor of the *Daily Orange*, which contributed to misunderstanding and diminished efforts to "celebrate diversity." Racial incidents, as reported in campus publications, fueled conflict. They began early in October 1989 with an overt racial incident in the campus library when two Black women "were verbally assaulted . . . when a White male shouted, "Shut the f___ up, niggers," and threw a book at them" (*Daily Orange*, October 19, 1989). The decision by the university Judicial Board was that the student "be placed on disciplinary probation until May 1990 and not on academic probation. In addition [he] must write an apology to the two women 'indicating a fuller understanding of the language that was used" ("Board decides on disciplinary probation," *Daily Orange*, November 2, 1989). As a result of this incident, a tone of disharmony was set for the entire year. Black freshman students were thus made aware of the hostile environment at this predominantly White institution early in their first semester.

Leon W. Chestang (1972), in an early article gave definition to the Black experience in the United States. The Black experience, he claimed, is characterized by three conditions: injustice, inconsistency, and impotence. Any place Blacks are personally made aware of "social injustice," incur "inconsistency of treatment" just because of their race, and are treated differently, thus experiencing the "feeling of impotence," may be considered a "hostile environment" psychologically. These Black students perceived their experience, albeit educational, to have occurred in a hostile environment.

The data for this book are riddled with anecdotes of the ignorance and insensitivity of the European American students. Black students used combat metaphors to describe preparing to go to campus. Perceptions of barriers and stereotyping judgments caused students to doubt their own ability, resulting, in some cases, in a self-fulfilling prophesy. Instances of racism were related as occurring in all phases of the student experience: residence halls, classrooms, campus offices. Perpetrators of these acts were not seen as "demons" or "devils" as we might be led to believe by the media. No, students called it insensitivity and ignorance. They viewed the campus as a "microcosm of the real world," as one student put it. Another called the campus a training ground for life in the real world.

2

✣ Social Context in the Early 1990s

Syracuse University, a major predominantly White institution located in New York State, gave considerable attention to recruitment and retention of students from previously underrepresented groups during the decade from 1980 to 1990. One approach, described as The Lubin House Experience, was used to attract urban minorities from the New York City area, New Jersey, and the New England states (Morrison, 1989). Successful recruitment efforts evidently do not ensure either successful enrollments or graduation rates. "Clearly, at the national level, aggregate Black enrollment in higher education has been in sharp decline. . . . Blacks are the clear losers" (Deskins, 1991).

In 1990, African Americans, who made up 9.6% (1,223,000) of the total college enrollment (13,710,150), received 5.8% (61,074) of the 1,046,930 baccalaureate degrees awarded nationwide. The percentage for *all* minorities *receiving* bachelor's degrees in 1990 was only 13.1% (166,641). According to the American Council on Education report on Minorities in Higher Education, this represents an increase of 5.8% (7,542) in the bachelor's degrees received by minorities from 1989 to 1990 (Carter & Wilson, 1992).

When we look at the ten-year picture (Table 2.1) of enrollment in higher education, it becomes clear that enrollment growth does not happen in a linear fashion. Note, for example, the decline from 1982 to 1984 and the small increase from 1984 to 1986 along with, a more significant increase from 1988 to 1990 (*Chronicle of Higher Education, Almanac* 1992). Deskins (1991) noted that for all degree levels (comparison 1975–1976 and 1984–1985), the percentage of degrees earned by Blacks was below their proportion of the total population. The statistics presented herein, like any statistics, may be suspect in that the sources used do not represent any uniform method of reporting.

Table 2.1	BLACK UNDERGRADUATE ENROLLMENT 1980–1990					
	1980	1982	1984	1986	1988	1990
ALL	1,107,000	1,101,000	1,076,000	1,082,000	1,130,000	1,223,000
Male	464,000	458,000	437,000	436,000	443,000	476,000
Female	643,000	644,000	639,000	646,000	687,000	747,000
4 Year	634,000	612,000	617,000	615,000	656,000	715,000
Private	231,000	228,000	232,000	228,000	248,000	271,000

Source: *Chronicle of Higher Education*, August 26, 1992

The following table gives us a snapshot of the Black and minority enrollment in 1988 and graduation figures for four years later in 1992.

Table 2.2	FOUR-YEAR GRADUATION FIGURES			
Undergraduate Enrollment 1988		Degrees Conferred by Racial Group 1992		
			Black	White
Black	1,039,000	Men	26,956	429,842
White	8,907,000	Women	45,370	506,929
TOTAL	11,304,000	TOTAL	72,326	936,771

Source: U.S. Department of Education, *Chronicle of Higher Education Almanac*, 1992, 1994

Deskin (1991), in his analysis of the ten-year period from 1974–1984, looked at enrollment and graduation rates of minority groups by region in the United States. He found that enrollment patterns "serve as reasonably good predictors of future outcomes" over time. Since 1984, the enrollment picture indicated increases in Black male and female students nationally. According to *Minorities in Higher Education,* although the enrollment figures were up, the percentage of total bachelor's degrees awarded to African Americans had declined (Carter & Wilson, 1992). Attention to the "quality of life" on campus, both academic and social, can have a significant effect on graduation outcomes and can make a difference in future graduation statistics. Institutions are being challenged to take a critical look at what is happening with their student populations. Who is getting in? Who completes their degree? Who is dropping out, and why?

In the 1970s and 1980s, many studies regarding Blacks in higher education were related to integration and adaptation as a result of desegregation and the Civil Rights Movement (Willie & McCord, 1972; Gruin & Epps, 1975; Ogbu, 1978; Blackwell, 1981; Fleming, 1984). In 1975, Vincent Tinto (1986) first postulated his theory of student departure, which stated that a student's persistence in higher education was related to the degree to which a student was integrated into the college's social and academic communities. African American and other Black scholars, researchers over the last 20 years (e.g., Wille & McCord, 1972; Gibbs, 1973; Ogbu, 1978; Fleming, 1984; Spencer et al., 1985; Fordham & Ogbu, 1986; Irvine, 1991), from disciplines such as psychology, anthropology and education, have studied reasons why Black children, at all levels of education, have difficulty learning, adjusting, and staying in predominantly White institutions. Much of this literature had not been considered in sociological studies of retention or attrition (Ogbu, 1978; Blackwell, 1981; Willie, 1981; Fleming, 1981; Astin, 1982; Thomas, 1984; Stikes, 1984; Allen, 1984; Asante & Noor Al-Deen, 1984; Nettles, et al., 1985; Richardson & Bender, 1985). Other scholars—many testing Tinto's model—contend that there is a strong relationship among attitudes, intentions, behavior, and how students manage a new (college) environment (Ajzen & Fishbein, 1972, 1977; Bentler & Speckart, 1979, 1981; Bean, 1983). More recently, John Weidman, (1989) and John P. Bean (1990) suggested models that look at the external factors such as family encouragement, high-school peers, community support, and how the strength of the students' background plays a significant role in affecting socialization behavior on campus. Scholars have also begun to look at the consequence of the special treatment of Black athletes in higher education (Adler & Adler, 1991). In the 1990s, several African American and other scholars of color have written articles and edited anthologies presenting the multiple and historical perspectives on issues affecting Blacks' interaction in higher education (Lang & Ford, 1988; Allen et al., 1991; Altbach & Lomotey, 1991; Gibson & Ogbu, 1991; Willie et al, 1991).

Pascarella and Terrenzini's (1983) nine-year study of attrition among Black and White students indicated significant, positive association of academic and social integration to persistence among both groups of students. Mow and Nettles (1990) in their study of minority student access, persistence, and performance suggest that "Satisfied and academically integrated students have good peer relations and few interfering problems, perceive the university as nondiscriminatory, and perform relatively well in college." (p. 77). More recently, Tinto, (1994) having conducted research on communities in college settings, emphasized the centrality of the classroom experience and the imperative for institutions to create a climate in which multiple college communities can thrive.

Referring to the theory of "institutional fit" discussed by Alexander Astin (1975, 1982) and Cope and Hanna (1975), Astin found that minorities with the best chance of persistence had six characteristics:

1. high entrance GPA and test scores;
2. well-developed study habits;
3. a high academic ability self-esteem;
4. a relatively affluent, well-educated family background;
5. an integrated high school experience;
6. no outside job.

Astin's findings were based on Cooperative Institutional Research Program (CIRP) survey data from students' first two years of undergraduate work. Data gathered from my students, who entered college in 1989 and graduated in 1993 and 1994, help us to develop a better understanding of how these characteristics play out during the four years to graduation. The last two years were a more decisive period in my study of persisters. Students' data indicate that it was during the fifth through seventh semesters that life decisions were made after getting to know themselves and coming to grips with their Black identity—being Black and knowing themselves, their worth, their responsibilities in this predominantly White world.

There is also the area of psychosocial development of traditional college-aged students which suggests that there are natural developmental processes students go through (Chickering, 1969, 1993; Cross, 1978, 1991; Perry, 1970, 1981). For the African American population of this study it was necessary to look at the literature on "Black Identity" and "coping skills" of minorities in a majority culture (Fleming 1981; Spencer et al, 1985; Fordham & Ogbu, 1986; Helms & Parham, 1990; Cross, 1991).

Many student characteristics have been overlooked by researchers using current models that explain attrition and persistence (Pascarella & Terenzini, 1991). Sociologically based research on student persistence places emphasis on the general socialization process in college rather than on the attributes of the individual undergoing socialization (Weidman, 1989). *Social integration* is a factor that describes student participation in campus clubs or organizations, and includes their discussions of personal problems with faculty and peers and their career-planning strategies. Nettles (1988) emphasized that "students with high social integration have lower grades but they graduate in a shorter period of time" (p. 27). In a later study he substantiated that the in-college behaviors of students, of Black and White students of both sexes, along with the institutional environment, have the greatest effect on student socialization (Nettles & Johnson, 1987). I found, that among these Black students campus socialization is a deciding factor contributing to student resolve. The issue of where the student lived on campus was discussed as part of developing their identity. It stands to reason that the students' perspectives should also be investigated to understand the nuances of the psychosocial development of African American and ethnic students.

The Summer Institute—The Pre Experience

Syracuse University, through the Division of Student Support and Development, sponsors several programs for the encouragement, enrichment, and academic support of students from under represented ethnic groups. Preeminent among these programs is the Summer Institute—a comprehensive precollege experience (The Summer Institute program was modified in 1990 and again in 1998 when the name and criteria for qualification were changed. It is currently "The Summer Start Program"). The Summer Institute was the "umbrella" organization administered through the cooperation of both the Center for Academic Achievement Counseling and the Student Support Center.

The Summer Institute (SI) of Syracuse University is a "six week transition program conducted during the summer prior to the freshman year" (Yonai, 1991, p. 11). The Summer Institute is a unique experience: An array of resources and services are available to the students including courses, academic advising, orientation, tutoring, career planning and counseling. Conceived in 1979 as an addition to the New York State-funded HEOP, this precollege program is a compensatory education program whose mission is to provide a true educational opportunity to students of prior disadvantage (H. Smith, 1991). Students in this program represent diverse racial and ethnic backgrounds; however, "they shared an important common experience, economic deprivation" (H. Smith, 1991, p. 53). In 1991, Horace Smith noted that the Summer Institute was developed, "around the concept of developing skills for the purpose of student empowerment. Students were viewed as learners in an environment which was likely to be insensitive and minimally receptive of their presence." Little has changed over the past fifteen years in the basic philosophy of student empowerment although the criteria for inclusion in the six-week summer program was changed in 1998 to allow more students to benefit from early orientation.

My interest in collecting data for this study has been to find out "how individuals create and understand their daily lives—their method of accomplishing everyday life" (Bogdan and Biklen, 1982). I have tried to learn how Black students accomplish their everyday lives with regard to their socialization, learning, and being on a predominantly White campus. I see them as active meaning makers who persisted in a higher education setting perceived as hostile to them. How they learned, practiced, and made sense of the dynamics of power, particularly the constant or ruling relations of race, becomes the focus of my investigation. I wanted to contextualize and analyze the experience of these young adults both collectively and individually. Collectively as a heterogeneous group (perceived as a monolith called "minority group") and individually coming from different backgrounds with different skills, what coping skills do these students bring and/or develop to survive and succeed in a hostile environment?

Researcher as Instrument

Central to any research is the role of the researcher. This research provided a unique situation. Consider an African American student interviewing another African American student. Seemingly such an interview would be very simple to carry out. It would seem to be easy for the interviewer to establish rapport with the interviewee. In this case, however, the researcher was an older African American woman, seeking to interview students also of the African American diaspora between the ages of eighteen and twenty-four. It was not easy, even though there was a similarity of cultural background, because there were differences in age, experience, and circumstance.

I began my undergraduate career only after rearing my family. Consequently, I do not have the same frame of reference for life on a college campus as the students in my study. Upon entering college in 1983, I was not a typical young adult between the ages of eighteen to twenty-four going off to college. I had never lived in a residence hall, nor had I ever had to address a professor from an immature stage of intellectual development (although I have had encounters with professors as a mature woman). I was afraid that I could not consistently compare my participants' experiences to my own. As a Black woman and a mother of college graduates, I have assumptions of what the African American college student might be experiencing. There is little, if anything, I can do about my assumptions except to recognize and remain sensitive to how they might affect my research and conclusions. To that end, I acknowledge some preconceptions about the values that these students bring to campus: personal pride, dignity, and a sense of accomplishment in their own community. The extent to which the data support these assumptions will be discussed in succeeding chapters.

In 1988, I was hired as an administrator in the Syracuse University Events Office that served as the liaison office for departments and student organizations to schedule their nonacademic events, i.e., meetings, colloquia, symposia, and entertainment, as well as the services necessary to facilitate these events. In the role of Events Manager, I met a number of students, particularly student leaders, who needed to schedule events. These students, representing different organizations, various ethnic groups, and all levels, from freshman to senior, visited my office to schedule their events.

A year and a half later, in August 1989, I received a fellowship to pursue my master's degree in Public Administration full-time at the university. While working on my master's degree, I decided to continue into the Ph.D. program in Higher Education, primarily to learn to observe and research college students. Specifically, my interest was in African American students because of situations I had observed in my capacity as Events Manager working with student leaders. Black and Hispanic students, particularly, seemed always under pressure, always stressed out, but they were very positive in their roles as leaders trying to accomplish their goals.

When, as a student, I went out among other students on campus, I noticed that many Black students would walk across the campus as if they were carrying heavy loads, troubled, without the smiles on their faces that I expected of young college students. They appeared to have some serious matters on their minds. Nonetheless, when you approached them, they seemed to represent themselves in an upbeat, more cheerful manner. There seemed to be a sense of determination to control how they were perceived. I wanted to understand their college experiences. I talked to three or four of them during that semester (spring 1990), and they related their frustrations with campus bureaucracy, social interactions, and in just coming to campus each day. At that time, I was not doing any research. They were just confiding in me as an older, wiser student.

How I Came to This Research

In July 1989, the Summer Institute (SI), the precollege transition program, brought in and housed 92 students who would be entering the university's various programs in the fall as freshmen. Among those 92 students were the African American students with whom I began my pilot study. In an administrative capacity that summer, I hired some of these same students as work-study students in the Schine Student Center. That Fall semester, I became a full-time graduate student on the same campus. My continued enrollment over several years enabled me to observe those students who persisted for the entire four years they were in college—Fall 1989 through spring 1993.

From the time I began thinking about the question of how African American students persist, an additional concern was how to choose which students to ask, without merely pulling a random sample. One of my professors, during a conversation, mentioned a student, employee, Barbara Yonai, who had recently (1991) defended her dissertation: "The effects of a pre-freshman summer bridge program on student persistence into the sophomore year," which indicated that the students who came in the summer were given a good foundation and were the least likely to drop out. My professor suggested that a conversation with the author of that study might be time well spent.

Shortly thereafter, I met with Barbara Yonai to discuss her procedure and findings. Yonai's interest was in attrition of "at-risk" students who had taken the SI precollege experience. Hers was a quantitative study, to test the Tinto model of student persistence among SI students in the second semester of their freshman year, comparing them to a group of students who did not have that bridge experience. She encouraged me to solicit the qualitative data the African American students seemed willing to share. Their willingness to share was evidenced, she said, by student responses to the open-ended questions on the survey instrument she had used, as well as informal conversations she had had with various students.

My next step was to secure permission to conduct a pilot study from the Division of Supportive Services. This office was responsible for the SI program. The Director of SI program made available the roster, and copies of the archived journals of those students who were enrolled in the 1989 cohort. He offered his services and suggested that I also talk with other program staff.

3

✣ Student Development/Black Student Development

> *There is no one way to be Black.* Being Black involves a wide spectrum of thoughts and orientations.
>
> Cross, 1991; italics in original

Race is and must be considered the central component for the *Black Student Experience* (West, 1993). This is revealed time and again in the students' interview data as well as in the campus documents reviewed in this study. Three basic tenets of this book are:

- that all college students, between 18 and 24 years of age, experience developmental changes during their college tenure from first year to senior graduation, and
- that all college students experience developmental changes from adolescence to adulthood; and
- that in addition to the above two tenets, Black college students are also confronted with their Black identity and what it means in the larger community of the college campus.

Taking the first tenet of how all students develop, there have been several theories that have emerged and stood the test of time. Erikson a forerunner in formulating theory on growth and development (1964, 1968), posits three elements that form the basis of the theories of social, psychosocial and moral development used to understand student change over time. These elements enable us to view development from several different perspectives. Very broadly, the elements are:

1. the "epigenetic principle," which suggests the notion of a sociological clock, a biological clock, and a psychological clock that accounts for the development of character as affected by an individual's personal environment;
2. the concept of developmental tasks or "crises" that are characteristic of a stage or time of decision;
3. the specification of the "identity versus identity confusion" stage as the medial in healthy development. Cognitive processes continue as the person matures.

From a Black perspective, the sociological, biological, and psychological clocks have been set and affected by historical and economic circumstances that were not in the best interest of Blacks. Developmental "crises" for Black students are triggered earlier in life because of the color of their skin as they learn to live in White America through the school systems. They learn coping mechanisms in order to progress. Irvine (1990) in an earlier work discussed how students read teacher expectations.

The fact that college-aged students develop and that college does indeed have an effect on students have both been well documented (Chickering, 1969; Perry, 1970; Cross, 1978; Pascarella & Terenzini, 1991). I wanted to explore how these student development theories could be used to explain the experience of the Black students in my study.

College impact theories/models are regularly used to account for student withdrawal or persistence behavior in higher education. Of these models, the most frequently cited in the past twenty years has been the Tinto model (1975) of institutional departure. Vincent Tinto revisited his model in 1986, noting that there are five types of theories that helped to explain student dropout, interaction, and experience on college campuses: psychosocial, organizational, societal, economic, and interactionist. Of these he stated that the *psychosocial* theories emphasize the role of individual psychological attributes in the process of departure/withdrawal decisions. *Organizational* theories stress the effects of the organization on student behavior, whereas *societal* and *economic* theories look at the impact that external society and economic forces have on the process of student departure. Finally the *interactionist* theories see involvement of both student and environmental forces affecting outcome decisions that students make (p. 360). Tinto had reservations about each type of theory.

After discussing the types of theorists, and the shortcomings of each, Tinto argued for the interactionists who "take student behavior as reflecting both individual and organizational attributes" into consideration. Therefore the student leaving, "necessarily reflects the interpretation and meaning that individuals attach to their experiences within the institution" (pp. 365–366). At this point Tinto suggested that researchers take a longitudinal look at the student and the stages he/she goes through to become a part of the community of the institution. Tinto, in his book *Leaving College* (1987), identified three transitional phases (based on the work of Van Gennep) in the process of student persistence in college as:

1. separation from communities of the past;
2. transition between high school and college;
3. incorporation into the society of the college.

Tinto also made the point that "it should not be assumed that these stages are always as distinct and as clearly sequenced as we have made them." (p. 94). Black students in the current study felt that they had made transitions before coming to the university and that being ethnically different was both a challenge and a learning experience. What are some factors that intervene during the college period? What are some of the characteristics Black students bring to the environment, and how are these changed as transitions are made? Looking at student development theories is one way that researchers have since discussed the impact of colleges on student behavior

(Weidman, 1989; Pascarella & Terenzini, 1991; Murguia, et al., 1991; Cabrera, et al. 1992).

John Weidman (1989) looked at college impact as a four stage socialization process: anticipatory, formal, informal, and personal. He explained these stages as happening over time:

1. Anticipatory socialization—the acquisition of values and skills one perceives needed to obtain membership in a group. This stage happens as the student identifies, prepares for, and applies to colleges and universities.
2. The formal stage occurs when the individual meets the official criteria for acceptance.
3. The informal happens once the student is on campus and begins to make adjustments to try to meet unwritten, perceived expectations for membership into the larger group.
4. In the personal stage the individual begins to understand the totality of expectations, formal and informal, as they align with personal orientations and the student assumes membership and becomes part of the group setting the norms.

A fifth stage, unspoken by Weidman, is associated with the longing for acceptance by the larger group, such as occurs in each successive classroom. Based on data in this study, Black students found traversing these stages fraught with rule changes, misunderstandings, stereotyped notions of behavior and, in many reported cases, opted not to continue the process to full membership.

As Weidman discussed college socialization, he challenged the organizational structures of higher education, as well as considering students' interpersonal processes. The essence of this approach is summarized thus:

> Just as students differ in their patterns of interaction and personal orientations upon entrance, colleges differ in their structuring, intentionally or not, of both normative contexts such as student residences and classrooms, and of opportunities for social interaction among college students, faculty, and staff. (p. 297)

John Weidman posed the following queries, pertaining to *social interaction*: "What are the interpersonal processes through which individuals are socialized?" Pertaining to *organizational structure*: "What are the various characteristics of higher education institutions as socializing organizations that exert influences on students?" (p. 297). Further, he contends that "it is reasonable to assume that performance in college may be affected by the student's ability to cope with problems at home and other community settings" (p. 300). This coping with problems extends to "home" within residence halls. Because Weidman considers socialization a cumulative process, he incorporates past and present settings, and significant others into his model. He advocates longitudinal studies over the college experience of four years or more.

Murguia, et al. (1991) introduced ethnicity as a consideration in the student persistence model. In their study of Hispanic and Native American students, they explored the role of ethnicity in the Tinto model. They reconstructed the concept of social interaction and introduced *ethnicity* as "an important conditioning element in the social integration process." Murguia, et al. (1991) identified three concepts that describe the functions of ethnicity summarized as self-identity, a sense of place in the world, and affective support. Ethnicity serves to define self-identity and is a source of stability in the face of constant change and provides a sense of pride and security. The ethnic construct that the students in this study spoke of was "Black" because they said the university lumped them all—because of stereotypes—into one group called African Americans, even though this label was not true as the ethnicity of some of the students.

Theories/Models

Ernest Pascarella and Patrick Terenzini, in *How College Affects Students* (1991), employed developmental models and theories to discuss what happens to individual students between the ages of 18 and 22 using the terms *change* and *development*. As clarification, they offered these definitions: "*Change* refers to alterations that occur over time in students' internal or affective characteristics" (p. 16). It can be both quantitative and qualitative; it encompasses regression and progression; and it is a descriptive, value-free term. Change is not to be feared, only to be accepted as inevitable in life.

It is the transitions that cause the anxiety normally attributed to change (i.e., Black students in a predominantly White institution). Conversely, *development* is said to be systematic, organized, and progressive giving the presumption of growth or potential for growth. Development moves "toward maturity, toward greater complexity through differentiation and integration" (p. 16).

As I use three of the older theories of change—Chickering's seven vectors psychosocial model, Perry's model of intellectual and ethical development and Cross's theory of nigrescence (see figures 3.1–3.3)—my basic assumption is that these theories have elements in common with each other. Developmental theories first, seek to identify the dimensions and structure of growth; second, explain the dynamics by which growth occurs; and third, view development as general movement toward greater integration, differentiation, and complexity in the ways that individuals think, value, and behave. As these theories have been designed, they indicate that movement is orderly, sequential, hierarchical, and that progress is continuous and gradual, not disjointed or abrupt.

Chickering's Seven Vectors

7. Developing Integrity
6. Developing Purpose
5. Establishing Identity
4. Developing Mature Interpersonal Relationships
3. Moving Through Autonomy Toward Interdependence
2. Managing Emotions
1. Developing Competence

Figure 3.1 CHICKERING'S SEVEN VECTORS
Source: Chickering & Reisser, *Education and Identity,* 2nd ed. (1993).

Since 1969, Chickering's theory of Seven Vectors of General Development has been accepted as the process by which students traverse from adolescence to adulthood. The Seven Vectors (Figure 3.1) are widely used by student life professionals in developing programming for student orientation and transition to college life. The first-year student enters college unsure of him/herself in the new surroundings. As the semester and the years progress the student develops competencies, manages to control and express emotions, and moves through autonomy toward interdependence.

Developing mature interpersonal relationships is facilitated to some degree by institutional programs, formal and informal student groups and activities, as well as classroom interactions with peers and faculty. Students, male and female, reach a point in their development where they must confront themselves and their individual self-concept. They must establish their identity. This searching for self happens within the context of both academic and social life, within activities such as career exploration, selecting a major, running for office, or serving on university committees. All students develop and change as they match previous experience with college experience while making intellectual and ethical choices. Development theories explain and help us understand the growth of students primarily, but not necessarily, in the freshman and sophomore years (specifically Chickering's first four stages and Perry's first four or five positions).

In conjunction with the physical and emotional development, students develop in their thinking and reasoning skills. In 1970, Perry presented a Model of the Intellectual and Ethical Development of college-aged students (Figure 3.2). Perry used student talk to understand the development of students' reasoning processes.

During the first year and into the second, students depend on getting their "true" information from "authorities" (parents, faculty, administrators). Students do not assume that they have definitive answers, but they do begin to form some opinions. As they get involved in their different roles as a student, student leader, member of a group (both academic and social), students move away from their dualistic thinking that things are either right or wrong (positions 1 and 2) and into a more multiplistic position where they see that there is more than one "right" answer or solution including ones the individual student may have devised (Perry's positions 3 and 4 and Chickering's stages 1–3).

Perry (1970) also introduced the concepts of *temporizing, escape, and retreat,* whereby students seem to waffle back and forth between the dualistic and multiplistic frame of reference. Perry explained these positions thus:

> *Temporizing*: The student delays in some position for a year, exploring its implications or explicitly hesitating to take the next step.
> *Escape:* The student exploits the opportunity for detachment offered by structures of Positions 4 and 5 to deny responsibility through passive or opportunistic alienation.
> *Retreat:* The student entrenches in the dualistic, absolutistic structures of Positions 2 or 3. (p. 10)

Perry's Model of Intellectual and Ethical Development

Commitment to Relativism
    Position (7, 8, 9)

Relativism
    Position (5 & 6)
                    >*Escape*

Multiplicity
    Position (3 & 4)
                    Retreat<

Dualism
    Position (1 & 2)

Figure 3.2 PERRY'S MODEL OF INTELLECTUAL AND ETHICAL DEVELOPMENT
Source: Adapted from W. G. Perry (1970), *Forms of Intellectual and Ethical Development in the College Years: A Scheme.*

These conditions may be evident on campuses where we see students' exaggerated behaviors or the students who become introverted and withdrawn. Dropping out or "stopping" out of school could also be considered a manifestation of temporizing and an inability to establish one's identity on a college campus.

Generally, by the latter part of first semester or early second semester, students begin to understand the environment, have gained confidence that they can handle the course work, and have found friends with whom to associate (Chickering's vectors 3 and 4). Relationships depend upon where the student is developmentally. As the students enter a new institution they are looking for guidelines, rules to follow (not like the rules back home), and knowledge of how to maneuver in a college setting. Negotiating the system can be less traumatic if the policies and practices of the institution are clear and consistent with the understanding the students have from what they may have been told by parents or have read in institution literature. First-generation college students may be at a disadvantage in this instance if there is no significant person to tell them what to expect or look out for.

To my knowledge and based on the population of students I interviewed, many Black students still come to college as first-generation college students—either on one side of the family or both. They have fewer role models in their families to prepare them for college, the social environment, or the institutional climate. Without the benefit of role models or mentors, Black students' development during the college years would be expected to lag behind that of those students who make up the larger campus population. However, as I have said before as the second tenet of this chapter "all college students experience from adolescence to adulthood developmental changes" including Black students. To review adolescent to adult development discussed thus far I have put Chickering's (1969) Seven Vectors together with Perry's (1970) Model of Intellectual and Ethical Development in Figure 3.3 depicting development during the college years for some students. I acknowledge that there have been many models of development generated over the last thirty years which expand on and add to the literature on student development particularly that of women's development (see Chickering & Reisser, 1993, for a full discussion). Of interest to the current study is Black student development.

In particular, data in this study support the general developmental directions as posited by Chickering and intellectual and ethical development in congruence with the positions in Perry's model. However, Chickering and Perry submit that students make choices in relationships and, in integration into a community, based on their ability to take in and use information that, the researchers contend, is a sequential process with each skill building upon the strength of the previous one. (see Figure 3.3.)

Figure 3.3 A CONCEPTION OF ADOLESCENT TO ADULT DEVELOPMENT (A JUXTAPOSITION)

7. Developing Integrity   Commitment to
    Relativism

                                   (7, 8, 9)

6. Developing Purpose   Relativism

                                   (5 & 6)

5. Establishing Identity

                                   >Escape

4. Developing Mature   Multiplicity
    Interpersonal Relationships

                                   (3 & 4)

                                   Retreat<

3. Moving Through Autonomy
    Toward Interdependence

                         Dualism

2. Managing Emotions

                                   (1 & 2)

1. Developing Competence

Speaking of the development of Blacks, William Cross (1991) contends that for the Black student (as well as the Black adult), regardless of the chronological time in history, past or present, the (five) stages of personal Black identity (Figure 3.4) have not changed

> *Stage 1. Pre-encounter* depicts the identity to be changed; *Stage 2. Encounter* isolates the point at which the person feels compelled to change; *Stage 3. Immersion-Emersion* describes the vortex of identity change; and *Stage 4. Internalization,* and *Stage 5. Internalization-Commitment* described the habituation and internalization of the new identity.

<pre>
               Stage 5
      Internalization Commitment
               Stage 4
           Internalization
               Stage 3
         Immersion / Emersion
               Stage 2
              Encounter
               Stage 1
             Preencounter
</pre>

Figure 3.4 CROSS'S STAGES OF PERSONAL BLACK IDENTITY
Source: Adapted from W. Cross (1991), *Shades of Black*

Cross, in this later work, revised his original 1971 model—specifically the initial preencounter stage—after a review of 45 of the earliest studies of Nigresence where misinterpretations of data were found to indicate something different than what was reported. Admitting to his personal error, Cross (1991) summarized thus:

> Like other observers of Nigrescence in the early 1970s, I assumed that Negro self-hatred was an established fact; consequently, my model, and every Nigrescence model of the time, implied that the average Negro American was "self-hating and deracinated," and thus very much in need of identity change. Moreover, most of us made little distinction between personal identity (PI) and group identity, or reference group orientation (RGO), but

when we did, it was clear that we assumed that the identity to be changed showed damage at both levels. Consequently, my depiction of the identity to be changed was a recapitulation of Kenneth Clark's self-hating Negro—thus the title of my model, *The Negro-to-Black Conversion Experience*. (pp. 158–159)

In order to understand the full experience of the Black student on a predominantly White campus, I have chosen to integrate all three student development theories; see Figure 3.5, Shadows of the Black College Student Experience.

The Complexity of the College Experience

I see the three theories intertwined to provide a new conception of the experience of the Black college student. The following is my synthesis of Cross's (1991) model with Chickering and Reisser's (1993) and Perry's (1981) model in my depiction of the Black students college experience at a predominantly white institution (Figure 3.5).

Student development as has previously been depicted is inevitable regardless of race or any other group descriptor. Looking at the diagram, Black identity is an integral part of Black student development from adolescence to adulthood—the three models intertwined, focused on the Black experience. Black college students have been through the *Pre-encounter stage* prior to entering college whereby they understand that acquiring an education is the way to get ahead in this society, have gone through different kinds of anticipatory socialization (Merton, 1968, Weidman, 1989) and, of course, are aware of skin color differences. According to Perry's (1981) scheme of intellectual and ethical development, the first years of college are governed by dualistic perception. Things are perceived as either right or wrong, good or bad, and basically derived from "authority." Parents and school administrators are "right" in matters of education. The student follows the expectations of these authorities. During this time students could begin to experience the confidence—a *sense* of competence—one has in one's ability to cope and to achieve successfully what one sets out to do (Chickering, 1969). This is also a time when the Black student meets other Black and African American students from various backgrounds and inevitably begins to experience some of what Cross (1978) defined, in his earlier work, as the *Encounter stage*:

> Encounter entails two steps: first, experiencing the encounter and second, beginning to reinterpret the world as a consequence of the encounter. The second part is a testing position during which the individual cautiously and fearfully tries to validate his new perceptions (p. 17). Coming to the college campus may be the first time these students have confronted different interpretations of what it means to be "Black."

Shadows of the Black College Student Experience
(Synthesis of three models by RDDavis, 1996)

5. Internalization Commitment		Commitment to Relativism
7.	Developing Integrity	(7, 8, 9)
6.	Developing Purpose	
		Relativism
5.	Establishing Identity	(5 & 6)
4. Internalization		<Escape
4.	Developing Mature Interpersonal Relationships	
3. Immersion/Emersion		Multiplicity
		(3 & 4)
3.	Moving Through Autonomy Toward Interdependence	
		Retreat>
2. Encounter		
2.	Managing Emotions	Dualism
		(1 & 2)
1.	Developing Competence	
1. Preencounter		

Figure 3.5 SHADOWS OF THE BLACK COLLEGE STUDENT EXPERIENCE

Students come back to school the second year with some understanding of the campus culture; of what is expected of them academically and socially. They make the transition from a dualistic mindset to a more multiplistic way of thinking (Perry, 1981). (For some this transition may happen a semester or two later depending on the individual *and* circumstances.) The institution is no longer making decisions for them totally. Parents are seen as not knowing "what's going on" as the student sees it. Students are given the power to make choices in their class work, in their social lives, in declaring a major.

In seeking *autonomy* (Chickering, Stage 3), simultaneously Black students traverse the *immersion/emersion stage* of developing their Black identity (Cross, stage 3) as they concurrently transition through the stage of multiplicity toward relativism (Perry, position 4). This period, most often in the junior year, for most students is the time when they become aware of the changes they have been going through. Perry's position 4a–4b and Cross's stages 3 and 4 discuss this stage as one where major choices are made. Black students *temporize* when they experience incongruity with the campus culture. Many students exhibited retreat and escape behavior, poor choices, or feelings of failure before deciding to persist to graduation. Similarly, the Black student experiences dissonance as s/he meets the challenges, makes the decisions and, ponders the question, *Who am I?* in this new context. *Internalization* (Cross, stage 4) is where I see that Black students and all students, at Chickering's stage 5 and Perry's positions 5 and 6, are at the point of maturity where they become determined to graduate and do whatever is necessary even if it means another semester or another year.

I submit that the Black student's experience embodies the additional burden of finding his/her identity as a Black person. William Cross's theory, and his work with Janet Helms and Thomas Parham speak to this realization as does the subsequent work of several other scholars (Irvine, 1991; Steele, 1992; King, 1994; Hollins, 1994a) in the fields of psychology and teacher education. The extent of this discussion is beyond the scope of this report.

Contrary to prevailing notions (Fordham & Ogbu, 1986), Black students in this study did not arrive on the predominantly White campus with an intention to assimilate the White experience. Their expectations were as individual as the students themselves. Cross explains, "*There is no one way to be Black.* Being Black involves a wide spectrum of thoughts and orientations" (italics in original, p. 149). However, students in this study were all expecting (1) to graduate with a degree in four years; antithetical to current higher education rhetoric, Black students, as I know them, still expect a college education to be a four-year degree program except for athletes who, because of an additional year of athletic eligibility extended to them by way of a practice known as "Red-shirting," expect to graduate in five years; (2) to make their families and communities proud; and (3) to get involved with other students "who are like me." This phrase proved to have multiple meanings even among this small group of Black students.

As they relate to the Black student who enters college, Cross's stages explain the inevitable changes our young people face as they attempt socialization primarily with other Black students, and students of color in an effort to be "connected, accepted and affiliated."

William Cross emphasized, however, that having a sense of connection and affiliation is not necessarily the same as having a *Black Identity*. A Black person can find and have a sense of connectedness with a reference group which has little to do with their nationalism or Black identity, e.g., church, profession, sport, political party and, in a college setting, educational philosophy. Cross explains in his 1991 book, *Shades of Black*:

> The reference group functions of Black identity lead to the celebration of Blackness, the press to solve Black problems and a desire to promulgate Black culture and history. At its worst it provides the basis for inhibiting, if not destructive, social conformity, ethnic chauvinism, reactionary cultural ideologies (biogenetically based ideologies), and a tendency to view as less than human, to one degree or another, those who are not "Black"—such negative and positive potential accompany any and all forms of nationalism,

ethnicity or group affiliation, and is thus not unique to the Black experience, one can embrace a cultural perspective without being reactionary, but all biogenetically defined notions of culture are inherently reactionary. (p. 217)

Where I reinterpret the Chickering, Cross, Perry theories (see Figure 3.6), I found that the *Establishing Identity vector* and the

**The Black Students' College Experience
at a Predominantly White Institution***

5. Internalization Commitment
GOAL CLARIFICATION
Personal Commitment

4. Internalization
ESTABLISHING IDENTITY
GOAL ASSESSMENT
Accepting "Who I am"; Commitment to self

3. Immersion/Emersion
IDENTITY CONFUSION
Searching for understanding of self;
Affirming one's Blackness

2. Encounter
DIVERSITY INQUIRY
Sees the college campus as a melting pot

CAMPUS INCONGRUITY
Sees the world as Black and White

1.   Preencounter

Figure 3.6 THE BLACK STUDENTS' COLLEGE EXPERIENCE AT A PREDOMINANTLY WHITE INSTITUTION
*An explanation of this model is included in chapter 7.

Internalization, and the Relativism stages aligned most closely. That is, students enter a position of personal discovery and decision making a comfort zone whereby things are taken in context as they relate to the individual students and their circumstances. Based on data from this study, Black students experienced these developmental phenomena between the second semesters of the sophomore year through the senior year. Given the individual Black student and her/his personal background (social and familial and academic) characteristics, the decision to move from internalization (stage 4) to internalization commitment (stage 5—Black identity) reinforced their decision to persist to graduation or to take another path.

Students in my study had mixed emotions about the experiences. One thing I noticed was that in earlier (1991) interviews there was more anger and indignation about what students perceived as racist and differential treatment than when second interviews were conducted in 1993. As mentioned above, student interviews were begun during the sophomore year and that the students were in transition from adolescence to adulthood. Students talked about being African American, the meaning of their heritage, and mistreatment in a way that implied that this was new knowledge, indicating culture shock. Each student had cultural distinctions from, and cultural connections to, the other Black students.

In the second interviews that took place in the spring and summer of 1993, most students were in their senior year, the comments were much more reflective and understanding of both sides of the institution/faculty perception, and the student's personal perceptions. Students' reflections were suggestive of reasons why situations exist and an understanding that changes were not eminent. Cross (1991) and his colleagues (Helms and Parham, 1990) indicate that at this point the Black student has returned to the "baseline" where race is of low salience. It is clear that the "baseline" is not the same for all people of African descent because we are not one monolithic group.

In the data of this study, race was never "of low salience." Students reported that the significance of race, both positive and negative is what made their college experience most memorable. Once students felt comfortable with themselves, they were able to make decisions about friends, classes, careers, and service to their Black community. Establishing and accepting their Black identity allowed the students to feel good about themselves and their goals to complete their academic programs and graduate.

A PERCEPTION...

As I wait at the bus stop
seeing all shapes of sistahmothaaunties
going to work; to play
Just going, going, going . . .
With a smile or a word of encouragement
"Stay in School Girl"
"I bet yo' momma prouda you!"
Their souls whisper
Stay in school for us
so they will know who we are
where we've been, what we know.
Tell our story
From our tawny- carmel corn - cafe au lait
to our onyx and ebony
so they <u>will</u> know
what [Blacks' persistence] look like.

From "What Is a Feminist?" by Angela Williams (1995). Angela completed this poem while weathering the storms of racism at a second predominantly White university. Poem by permission of author, previously published in Davis 1996.

4

❦ The Campus As the Black Students See It

The students in my study were interviewed in their sophomore year and again in their senior year. These Black and African American students were asked to reflect on all of their years at the university. The open-ended nature of the questions allowed the participants to answer from their own frame of reference rather than from one structured by prearranged questions (Bogdan and Biklen, 1982). More focused questions were asked during the second interviews with nine of the eighteen students. Second interviews were done when students were in their last year of school. Students remembered quite vividly their first visits to university property, their excitement, and their apprehension. The statements included in this chapter represent the Black *students' perceptions* of their experiences at a predominantly White institution.

The reflections of study participants, in this chapter, encompass the early years and initial feelings as the students made choices of friends, programs, and organizations, and their own behavior in this new environment. Students' initial concerns were not about the academic work ahead. Research on the college student (Fleming, 1984; Nettles, 1985; Allen, et al, 1991; Davis, 1991; Pascarella & Terenzini, 1991; Cabrera, et al., 1992;) has shown that students have many concerns which, although not classified as academic, do, nevertheless, have a significant bearing on their ability to accomplish their academic work. Jacqueline Fleming (1984) in *Blacks in College* noted that "Cognitive growth . . . appears to have many facets, all of which are undoubtedly influenced by a variety of nonintellectual factors" (p. 191).

Initial Impressions: *Campus Visits and Preorientation*

First visits to the University, for some students, were by invitation to a special weekend. These orientations were known as Black and Hispanic Weekend on the main campus. Some students attended a Minority Reception at The Lubin House, the university center in New York City. The Black and Hispanic Weekend was sponsored by the Admissions Office to bring minority prospects to campus for a preorientation to the many campus activities, both social and academic, that Syracuse University offered for minority involvement in the campus community. Gail, one of the participants in my study, felt that Black and Hispanic students should have been hosted during the week instead of the weekend: "I wish that we could have sat in on classes." She felt overwhelmed by the size of the introductory classes in the large lecture halls during her first semester, having come from a small Catholic high school in a small suburb of New Jersey. Routinely, during Black and Hispanic Weekend, the academic component was explained by discussion of programs and a tour of the physical space rather than any actual classroom visit. Students were able to get a sense of campus life. Johanna, another participant, however, had mixed feelings about the weekend but was reassured by the activism she witnessed:

> Oh [it was] great. It's good in a way and in a way it's not because you're focused on African Americans and your experience and all is something that is predominantly Black, but that's not really the situation here [in a regular semester]. So, when you get here, it's different. Aside from the fact that you have no work to do and you come for the weekend, you're just like, enjoying yourself. So, but it was good, it was good. I remember when I came there was a big controversy over the Science and Tech protests by the Student African American Society (S.A.S.). They [administrators] explained what had happened, and it was good to see that the students were aware and were activists and not passive, so you know that sparked my interest. (Johanna, intv #1)

During that weekend, each student was hosted by a minority student currently enrolled at the university and was encouraged to socialize with others. Johanna remembered having made an acquaintance on this weekend who became a sustaining friend once reunited on campus in the fall: "And I met up with someone I met during the Black and Hispanic Weekend. She's in the choir. She's my roommate now." The name of the Black and Hispanic Weekend has gone through a couple of changes after 1990 to be less stigmatizing. First it was changed to Minority Weekend and is currently Multicultural Weekend, serving the Black and Latino prospective students.

The evening Minority Receptions at The Lubin House were the first in a series of preadmission information activities that began for some students early in their junior year of high school. Receptions provided opportunities for students and their parents to interact with a university representative in New York City (Morrison, 1989). For many of these students, the cost of a visit to campus would have been prohibitive. Special nights in the local environment allowed parents and students to discuss salient issues such as housing, financial aid, admissions requirements, and student life. A pre-professional program information session was the other major component of The Lubin House experience. These sessions had a particular program focus (Morrison, 1989). Precollege activities provided an opportunity for under represented students to meet someone who could be that one familiar face in the sea of unfamiliar faces on campus in the fall.

Tirae—a sophomore at the time of the interview—gave her perception of why these preorientation meetings made a difference:

> We took placement tests to see where you are in math and so on and so forth. So down in The Lubin House in New York City, I had met everyone that I was to be in Summer Institute with. I don't know, for the most part, only one or two people didn't come to the Summer Institute. We had lunch together, so we had gotten to know one another before we came to Summer Institute. We had exchanged phone numbers so I had been speaking with some people before I actually got here. So by the time I got to Summer

Institute, I already had some friends. So by that time we were building on already started, already made friendships.

Friendship is a theme that surfaced through all of the students' data. Having made friends prior to coming in the summer made the choice of Syracuse University more exciting and the transition to college a little easier.

Choices—Why Syracuse?

Not all students mentioned the weekends or receptions. A number of students said they knew the school from its national sports reputation. Freddie, a student leader, was quite clear about how he made his choice to come to Syracuse:

> Well, coming to Syracuse, first I'll have to say that their Sports program is the main attraction, and I have become familiar with Syracuse University by watching Dwayne Pearl Washington play basketball for Syracuse. And from watching the team that he was playing, I became interested in the athletics and I decided that, given that this was already a favorite college basketball team, I decided to look into the academics offered by Syracuse University. And I discovered that Maxwell School of Citizenship was supposed to be one of the top schools in the country. Therefore, I figured that I couldn't lose by coming here and that's how I chose Syracuse University.

Freddie, however, was not an athlete and did not play any team sports once he came to Syracuse University. For some of the students, the reasons why they chose Syracuse was not as clear as for Freddie. What was important was that they had been accepted. Celeste who was a track star in high school related:

> I'm from New York City . . . once I found out I had got accepted to Syracuse, all the other colleges I applied to (I said), "Well it doesn't matter because I got accepted to a private school." I have no idea why I was so headstrong about going here but once I found out I was accepted, every other school kind of just fell by the wayside. I didn't really apply to very many predominantly African American colleges. I applied to Howard but I had no intentions of going there because my older sister had gone there and I didn't want to go where she had gone . . . once I got accepted here I was ready to

go, ready to come and be here all summer and all year. I was very intent on coming here.

Several students spoke about "being accepted" with pride because of what it meant for their family and community:

> . . . a lot of people, a lot of my friends back home, I have two friends who, one is in college and one isn't. Every time I come home like for the summer, we talk and hang out. I get the feeling that they kind of look up to me. They know that I am a really good student and they know that I am a good person in general.

The transition of leaving home and going to an unfamiliar place is a part of growing up. When college is that transition, there are associated feelings of excitement and apprehension. Yoclee described what it was like taking the road-trip from Manhattan to Syracuse to attend the 1989 Summer Institute:

> We came through the mountains and there's nothing (pause), but farm animals and White people. I said, "Oh mommy, no, no." But before I left [home], let me tell you, I cried. I cried the whole way up here. I cried myself to sleep.

Yoclee's statement was not meant to say that she did not know that Syracuse University was a *predominantly White institution*. She did; they all did. What most of them did not know, however, was what those words looked and felt like in actuality.

Housing and Roommate Selection

Students in this study had mixed emotions about coming to a predominantly White university, depending on their personal background and circumstances. Maria, a Biracial student from a small town in northern Pennsylvania, told how she chose which residence hall she wanted to be in that freshman year:

> I had a feeling. Is that strange? I had a feeling. I came up to the campus in the summer [1989], which is not an accurate time to come up to the campus.

> I asked people. I saw the way they printed up literature for the campus. I noticed, when I was picking out my housing after I was accepted, they had subtle ways of directing minority students where they wanted to put us. Sadler [residence hall] had a picture of an African American right beside the name. And no other place in the brochure was there an African American.

Maria chose that particular residence because she perceived that was where she would be with other students like herself. On reflection, four years later, her perception was that it was a subtle suggestion by the university in their advertising to house Black students in that building. Was Maria paranoid? Yoclee had a similar perspective on the housing on south campus. There were a large number of Black students who lived in one section of the south campus housing, particularly after their first year. It was not clear if this was coincidental, by design or by self-selection. Yoclee said:

> I lived there. There is a lottery system. That is what they say they have. They have a lottery system. I believe it is in the planning in the University. And then, you can say well that is where the Blacks choose to be among each other. But it still turns out to be segregated. No matter how you pick it. Why is that? I don't know. You tell me.

The majority of the Black students at the university moved either to south campus housing or off campus after their freshman year. During the years 1989–1993, however, the numbers of Black women living in the only all-female residence hall increased. Two of the women in this study lived in this particular residence hall all four years they were on campus. Johanna was not pleased with her first roommate situation there:

> I felt pretty bad . . . I did, because, I lived in Haven and they put me in a four-person suite with three White girls. So, it was like, it was hard. They were the only people I knew. So, it was like, we'd go to dinner, I'd be with them all the time because they were the only ones I knew and then on my floor, the people on my floor, they were just doing their own thing. They seemed to know each other already so, um, I'm kind of reserved so it was hard for me.

Racial issues were discussed at residence hall meetings. Gail remembered one such meeting where they discussed separatism:

> Um, yes, because, that would come up in floor meetings, you know. (someone said) "Well you seem unapproachable." You know, like "I feel threatened" and (I said) "You don't threaten me. Why are you threatened by me?" you know. Different interests, you know. (they said) "I can't relate to you as Black people." "I'll speak to you," I said and everything but I always felt... I mean, not intentionally, like, "I don't want to be with you because you're White." But, I couldn't relate. I don't know . . . Um, actually, I remember one [meeting] in the Spring semester. And the big thing was "You all eat together." It's like, well, "You all eat together too," you know. "It's not like we're separate. You're separating yourselves off." You know, [I said] "We're not going to yell at you if you come over" . . . but . . . .. It was always [them saying] "You're separating yourselves from us."

The students felt the hall meetings allowed them to voice their feelings, but the subject kept coming up. Johanna did get a Black roommate the following semester (Gail), who was of like mind and culture. They remained roommates until their graduation in 1993. Rema was also one of the students who commented on the university housing arrangement:

> I was like, 'Wow!' It never occurred to me until I came back (in the fall) and I was in Flint [Hall] on the 'Mount'. And usually they put all Black people in Sadler Hall and actually I'd love to get in Haven. But I was on the Mount because I guess I got lucky or whatever. So there were like [three] of us on the floor—me, my roommate and another girl who was in another wing, and she ended up being my third roommate sophomore year. It was so funny because there weren't that many of us. There were a couple [of Black students] in Day Hall. It wasn't that many of us. . . There were a couple of Latino people that summer, but they were trying to go for Whites.

Tirae explained her perception of the process of how Black students met other Blacks and also a bit of what it felt like to need another Black person and a certain level of comfort:

> I think the place where most of the Black students meet one another is probably the dorm at first. When you have the initial floor program and you

say, oh there is so and so. Or there is another Black person over there, and lunch and dinner are at such and such a time. Maybe she wants to go to dinner. So I think a lot of people they meet each other there. After that, I think it spreads to probably in areas like classes, the Schine [Student Center] and parties. I think it first begins where people need the most help, so to speak. When you first come into the university, you kind of need help because you are like, okay, "I am here by myself, I don't really know too many people," and people latch on to one another for support. So I think that is where the interaction begins. Afterwards, you start seeing one another in more social-type places and that is where you get to see who is about what and what is about who and what this person really wants to do, even though they said X, Y, and Z. You start seeing those things. I think that is when you can pick and pull and say, "I can only hang out with her when I am on this type of level." "We can't really hang out on this type of level" and things like that. So I think that is where most of the interaction between Black students begins.

We recognize that any college student needs friends and a comfort level to be able to settle down to the academic tasks at hand. What these students talked about were the challenges to being able to satisfy their basic needs. Basic needs may be met by either socioemotional or instrumental support (Davis, 1991). "All students need socioemotional support in the form of affection, sympathy and understanding, acceptance, esteem from others, and instrumental support considered as advice, information, help with academic problems and financial aid" (p. 155). For Black students, choosing to come together for a meal or a meeting gratified their socioemotional needs. Programs like the Summer Institute addressed their instrumental needs.

Summer Institute — Student Benefits

The Summer Institute program was designed to help students from socially and academically disadvantaged backgrounds to become familiar with college life and demands, before coming on campus in their first semester. The 1989 SI program was mentioned by students who were *not* in the program as well as those who participated. Nine of the eighteen African American students (four males and five females) in my study had attended SI program.

Celeste initially considered coming to the summer program a punishment, but she readily admitted to the lasting effects it would have on her interpersonal skills:

> I had no summer vacation at all, and I was very bothered by that but . . . I feel I definitely have grown from the experience. I've gotten a lot, aside from academically, as far as me as a person, I grew a lot from that experience because (pause) it was a challenge for me to have to bite my tongue a lot, and have to deal with authority figures.

Celeste was referring to the authoritarian structure and rules of the SI program at that time: structured study hours, structured meal times and even mandatory fun, e.g., the fourth of July picnic. Being the eldest and a track athlete in high school, she was used to being responsible for herself and felt the students were being treated like children. In spite of her displeasure at the time, she considered the experience valuable in the long run.

All eighteen students agreed that SI students had advantages over the other freshman going into the fall semester. Celeste explained a bit of the complexity of that advantage:

> The Summer Institute people. We knew where all the buildings were. We knew where not to go. We knew what was fun here. We knew places to go to hang out on the weekends. We had been up here for so long. . . We had a clique! And (pause) I noticed through my interacting with other people that it was kind of (pause) it was tighter than I really thought it was. Like, some people didn't fit in just because they weren't in Summer Institute and they had a harder time trying to hang around with us. A lot of the times, in my opinion, it depends on the school they come from. Like some people that came from small schools are overwhelmed by the size. Some people that come to Summer Institute feel that there's going to be so many African Americans when they come back that they're overwhelmed when they [return] in the fall.

Kasey told me that most of the students were from down in the New York City area. She said students came mostly from the same high schools "in Brooklyn and Queens, some from the Bronx." She explained them having a certain camaraderie because of coming from "The City." She said:

> There was only a few people from like, Buffalo, M__ was from Buffalo, my friend L__ is from Buffalo. And everybody else was from . . . ah . . . back home. There's like, just the boroughs, like Queens, Manhattan, Brooklyn. It's like "Oh, you used to hang out in the 'Red Zone.' Yeah, I used to be there too." And you find out that you used to club with the same people. You used to hang-out with the same people. That's basically it. Most of the people were from back home, which was surprising. I mean you just knew you'd come up here and meet a lot of people from different places . . . But I think Summer Institute, gave like a strong foundation as far as like getting people in contact when you first come here.

Rema helped me understand why the students formed cliques. It was not by a master plan or secret pact. It was the thing to do to try to make the best of the social time allowed in a very tight SI academic schedule. Rema explained:

> . . . [T]here were three people from my high school [in SI]. That is it! Everyone else pretty much got together. We had no choice, you know. We ate together, studied together, slept together, everything. We had no choice. The little time that we had after study hour, everybody just stayed together. So it was just like, you know, there was no not liking one another. We spent time together. It was a little cliquey because everybody had their own group pretty much depending on where you lived or what classes you had or who was with you. But basically my circle now is pretty much my circle from SI. [Also] a couple of people from my high school who came to Syracuse that I have known for years . . . But it's the same. My roommate now [senior year] was in Summer Institute with me.

A point to note is that both males and females in this study maintained throughout their college experience the friendship bonds made during those initial contacts with the institution. In some cases the students became roommates, they had a strong bond that allowed them to feel safe. Rema also referred to the fact that the six-week stay on campus at that time was structured very tightly to ensure that the students learned good study habits, how to relate to authority, how to compete in and assimilate into the campus community, and be prepared for college life.

These students obviously had a head start being familiar with the layout of the campus, but they also received other beneficial hands-on instructions during the summer. Tirae talked about the privileges of SI program that made them feel special:

> Also, probably the best in my Summer Institute was a class called REM (an abbreviated course prefix for "REMedial"). She [the professor] made us go to the library to learn how to use the library. Although the system has changed from the time I entered, I still know how to find things in the library. A lot of students don't know how to use the library. I think that was probably one of the greatest things I learned in SI because I was just walking in doing what I had to do and I was out whereas most people had to ask the librarian who had to take a lot of time to help (them).

Several of the students mentioned the teacher who taught the REM class that summer. (In 1990, the course prefix, REM, was changed to CLS to reflect the purpose and content of the college learning strategies class. This class is still a 3-credit, required course for all HEOP, SI students and is offered as an essential component of the Summer Bridge Program open to any in coming freshman or transfer student.) This teacher was a Black woman who, from a Black perspective, was realistic about the academic challenges of being a Black student on a predominantly White campus. Yoclee's perception summarizes the intensity:

> It was like a college preparation course and she was . . . She worked us overtime . . overtime and, her famous quote was "Y'all got to get y'all's shit together."[Yoclee stopped and broke out in a big laugh and was, it seemed, remembering some things around that phrase. It is a phrase that we use when emphasizing a resolve or something of consequence.] She continued with what that type of caring meant to her: Ah . . . and I loved her because she was so inspiring and I think, as an African American, we as African Americans need someone to push us a little bit more, a little bit harder, not be so lenient on us. She pushed us. And my experience with her, I didn't have a problem, just was run down and tired from my REM class but I . . . I don't regret it.

Although the REM class provided students with advanced knowledge of campus resources and opportunities for campus interaction, it was also stigmatizing as the remedial class for underprepared minority students required for every SI student. It is noted that many of the grant programs, scholarship and fellowship programs include other designated under represented groups (Hispanic, Native American, women, etc.) as do those that are based on economics alone. I use only the category Black here because that group is the topic of my study. This is not meant to imply that any of these programs are exclusively for Blacks.

Jay Jay, a male participant, believed that students gained more through SI than they could expect to garner on their own. The camaraderie and entree to the campus hierarchy and the office structure was what he felt gave him an advantage. Here is how he put it:

> Another thing it did was it brought people together that otherwise would come up here and be lost. Being in Summer Institute opened a lot of doors for me with the administration and socially. When you come up here and you know these people. You know them. You know who they are and you interact with them. [Being in SI] gives you a chance to get to know the buildings. You're not as lost. You get to know the system of SU, your classes, how things are (pause). Over all, it did help me.

Arnie, another of the SI students I contacted in 1991, turned out to be the last student I interviewed again in 1993. Something always seemed to come up to postpone our meeting. Finally, when we met and I asked him to "tell me about your experiences" (and we confirmed he should start at the beginning), he began and related the saga of his transformation:

> Yes, 1989. It was, well, when I came up here (from high school) I was very, very shy. I wasn't very talkative at all. So when I met these two students, they had to coach me. They said "Hello, my name is Tammy." "My name is Lisa." They kind of shocked me because I was like, I never knew anybody to come up to me and just introduce themselves to me. In New York City it is not like that. I was really, like wow! But that really helped me to open up a little. It taught me how to talk to people. I found that hard in high school.

> Summer Institute was a very great experience. It helped me get familiar with the campus. It helped me get familiar with college life as a start. In high school, I found it very easy to just. . . We had a test and all I would do was study the night before and do good. But I found very soon in college that you can't do that. Summer Institute helped me in trying to organize my time and my schedule because there is a lot more to do in college than in high school. You have to manage your time very well in order to do good. So I learned through the Institute.

Students who had *not* been in the summer program also commented on the advantages of the SI program. Johanna recognized what she had missed by not having attended that program. She described her first week on campus:

> A lot of people that I met that [Minority] weekend didn't come here so, it was like I didn't know anyone, and then I came like a day late . . . [I]t seemed as though I came a week late and everyone was already matched up in pairs and then (pause). It's really different when you don't go to Summer Institute because everyone that went they knew each other already and you wonder, "What's going on?" (pause) so I'm like, "How come these people all know each other already?" You know, like "What's going on?" But it was really different, and it took a while to get into the gist of things after getting up here for the fall semester.

Dano also had a difficult time connecting that first semester because, although he was from *the City*, he did not qualify under SI criteria to attend the program. He wished he could have come to the program, however:

> . . . I didn't need to come, but I kind of wished I did come for the summer program. I think it's an excellent program because it sort of takes away a lot of that initial shock that can mess you up later on, that initial shock that most people go through that first semester freshman year and then they're struggling second semester freshman year. A lot of my friends that were in the summer program really did well their freshman year, and they continue to do well. I think the summer program is something that I missed out on.

Dano's perception that SI students did well in their first years is a different perspective from the one these students shared with me during their interviews. His comment is related to the social climate and the ability to find a comfortable place, socially, to be able to focus on the academic aspects of college. Students talked about "belonging" and their search for a group. There was not any one space or group that satisfied all students, however. Students' needs were individual, even when they were in a group.

The College Experience
How They See Us...

Students talked about their experiences and the prevalence of race and racially motivated distractions to reaching the academic expectations set by the families and communities they had come from. Even those Black students who had had the same advantages as White students (i.e., educated parents, economic stability, social experiences, even prep school) seemed to be traumatized by the institutionalized racism they encountered. More than one student related how there was, ever present in the institution, the lower expectation for Blacks and their frustration and dismay at still being "the only" or "one of a few" Blacks in class. Gail shared her feelings:

> Well, my experience, as an African American ...of course, now in my classes, as I go higher up [in her major], I'll be the only African American in class. And that's sometimes sort of hard... you get to realize... I might have to work a little harder, you know, than anyone else. I mean I have the attitude anyway I want to work harder.

Why is it that Gail felt that she had to work harder, even though she was valedictorian of her class at a private high school?

Being "in the spotlight" heightened the awareness of difference that increased for these students as they went to their classes. Celeste put it this way:

> Seems like we're afraid to ask people for help academically sometimes. I think it's just pride. "I don't want somebody to know that I don't understand this." When people feel like they are faltering, it seems like they're afraid to take the initiative to say "I really don't understand this." And, in a university of this nature, where we're the "minority," we're kind

of pressured to do better than anyone else, because we're expected to fail anyway.

Yoclee understood that this situation existed also, but she saw it as one where the onus was on the faculty person to support the student. She shared her thoughts on how Black students are not supported:

> It is just the way. For example, I have African American friends who have had encounters with professors and they have told them well maybe you should think about changing your major, or maybe this just isn't for you. All they needed was a little help. You know, and this is what [the student] wants to do. It wasn't one of those things where they needed to drop out. They weren't failing that drastically; they just needed a little more help. Sometimes you just get the impression, as a Black woman I have to say, you just know when something isn't right because of the color of your skin.

Tirae shared the following perspective encompassing a broader view of what it is like to be visible even when you are not when she explained:

> Well, as I said, it is always a surprise to you. You expect it, but you walk in the classroom, and you are hoping that it is more than you or more than two other [Black] people that are in your major. You walk in and it is like, "Oh, I didn't win this time." But it is interesting because everyone knows who you are. So if you miss class one day, they are able to say (whether it be the TA, the Professor, the students that are five rows down from you that you don't even know), they will know, "Oh, you missed class on such and such day." They can tell you this. There would be no way for me to tell you Suzie, Jane or Mary missed class because there are just too many in the class. They know everything about you, they can probably tell you what you had on that day, because you are the only one there. It is kind of interesting because you really have no privacy in a sense. There was really no privacy in a class because you are the only one so everyone is always able to single you out. If you never speak in class, they know that also. If you got a wrong answer, they know that. If you always talk in class and you always have something to say, they will definitely know that and not only will they know that, the rest of their friends will know.

Johanna and Rema spoke on the issue of being put in the position of being the spokesperson for the African American race. Johanna said:

It's difficult, and you know there are statistics saying that students do better at Black colleges, and I can understand why that is. I mean, you know, you're in a classroom . . . like, I'm still, in one of my classes, I'm the only Black person in there. And it's like, people . . . if there is a Black issue or something, people are looking to you to be the spokesperson. You feel a lot of pressure and you just feel pressure in general just being in the class where you're the numerical minority. You're like . . . um, "What if I don't do well, my whole race is kind of". . . the whole weight of the world is put on your shoulders. And, um, it's hard and sometimes it's intimidating, you know, if people have more background knowledge than you do. "Why don't I know this," you know? It's some disparity on your part or something.

Johanna pointed to how absurd it is to think that one Black person could speak for all, as well as the reality that sometimes you don't have the information, and the doubts and concern that situation can cause.

Rema commented on being the only Black on a search committee for a faculty position and shared her internal discomfort with the choices she had to deal with:

I was the only African American and the only woman on the committee. It so happened that the only African American woman who applied for this position, I picked her. I chose her as my recommendation. I wasn't going to pick her, because I didn't want people to think I was picking her because she was Black. She was the best person, and it was sad that I had to think that.

Rema also shared a related but different perspective on the way White people behave because she is a Black person:

I think that White people in general don't know enough about African Americans or Latinos or anything. There are the ones who do know, and they are still kind of undermining when they talk to you because they know. "I am not prejudiced." "I know about African Americans." . . . At the same time, there are the ones that are on the other end. You don't know which are worse. In Flint [residence hall], there was this one kid. To this day, I will see Doug, and he will come up to me and tell me something about Black people or about Blacks and like, "Oh my God, I can't believe that they did this to this Black guy. It is so sad." Is that the only thing you can talk to me about? Just because I am Black? He always has to tell me that his parents adopted this Latin boy from Mexico and, "Isn't that wonderful that my parents did

Black Students' Perceptions

that?" What do you want me to say to you? [She mimicked] At the same time, there were people in the same group that were like, "Why does Arseneo [Hall] always have to have somebody Black on his [television] show every night?" Freshman year somebody asked me that. I was like, why is that a question? Who says "Why does Johnny Carson always have somebody White on his show?" Nobody says that. So why is it a question that Arseneo has . . . So there are people like that in management and everywhere on this campus. I get the little comments, you know. I get the mimicking of Black people and they think that they are being funny.

Tirae's comments articulated the need to be surrounded by people of your culture and the comfort you feel being in your own element. I asked her to clarify her phrase "being from your own element":

"Being from your own element, or being with your own element." I think what we were talking about was walking into AAS classes and seeing people that look like you. You were at home in those classes because you know that the person sitting next to you at least can relate to something you had been through in your life on some sort of level . . . Because for Black students, that is your outlet. (pause)

She went on to explain the importance of having familiar cultural articles in your surroundings:

[Others are] always saying how everything in my room is Black. I have a map of Africa. I have Malcolm X on my wall. I have a picture of Sister Soldier. Then I walk outside and I say, "Damn, there go the White snow and there go the White people." It is like culture shock every day. You are used to it, but it is culture shock every day. You live in your room and everything in there represents you, or it should represent you.

The issue of race, racism, and differences appeared in every context of the students' lives. Chapter 5 will deal more specifically with critical incidents and the students' perceptions of the campus climate.

How We See Ourselves . . .

Among Black students, many retreat from majors (careers) within their ability in math and science fields, such as engineering, chemistry, and the professional schools, because of self-doubt imposed by stereotypical practices that have become the norm in predominantly White settings.

This study included 6 Black students who entered the university in either engineering (3), pre-med (2), communications (1)—with scores high enough to be accepted without benefit of special programs—but who, by the end of their second year, had changed their major. Of course, there were multiple reasons for these students to make changes in their majors. The following are two of the males who originally thought they wanted to be engineers and found little support and often condemnation when they struggled to find a career choice.

Arnie was one such student who candidly told me about coming in feeling competent of his skills in math and science and what it felt like to have that confidence eroded:

> In September in the fall of 1989 I was a freshman in engineering. I did engineering because in high school I did well in math. I had a 95 average in math. Science was more like 85. So I figured since engineering was math and science oriented, I would give it a try. It turned out I had a lot of difficulty. A lot of classes I didn't like. I did not want to do the work. I didn't get anything out of the work. I just thought it was boring and it wasn't for me. But I spoke to a lot of the upper-class engineering students and they were telling me there were some more problems. "In the beginning a lot of the entry-level classes are going to be hard. Gradually as you go to the upper-level classes, it won't get really easy, but it will get a little easier." So I said maybe it is like the first semester of my first year and I am going to give it another semester. So my first semester I didn't do well. My second semester I continued and I still didn't do well, but I figured maybe it is just the first year. Maybe the second year I will start to do better and I will start to think more in terms of an engineer and it will come to me. But I found out that it didn't. I kept discovering these problems that I could not solve. I had tutors, I had upper-classmen, but I just found that I did not like it. I thought I would because I liked math and science in high school. But also because I thought that if I got a degree in engineering, I could make some pretty good money when I get out. . . . [M]y grades were suffering badly because of it. Unfortunately, I was removed from the engineering school.

Arnie was deflated and his confidence shaken because he took this all personally, to mean he wasn't good enough. He came back the second semester sophomore year on academic probation in the College of Arts and Sciences. He said: "[Liberal Arts] *was declared as my major. I didn't know what I wanted to do. That was frustrating.*"

On the other hand, J. R., having had a similar experience, held fast to his belief in himself, when he found he did not like engineering. He struggled with pressures from the Director of Minority Engineers and other Black engineering students who cajoled him to study harder, and told him that he would make a lot of money as an engineer. J. R.'s perception was:

> The only problem I have with that is that [the Director of Minority Engineers] was put in as the head of minority engineering program but he's not an engineer. So a lot of what he does, I mean, he wouldn't understand a lot of what you know an engineering student would go through, you know, and that was something that I wouldn't fault him for because he's taking a position, he's taking a job like anyone else and this is the role he's put on to do but I fault the University for hiring him to do that. You know, I think they should hire, for one, an African American for the program [this Director was an African American man], and for two, someone that is an African American engineer. It's not that hard to find. So, but that's not his fault but that is the University's fault doing that. So a lot of the pushing that he did wasn't so much geared towards, you know, that you should be understanding this material, you should do this or that, but it was geared towards engineers in making a certain amount of money in the future.

J. R. made the decision to change his major, moving from Engineering to Arts and Sciences in Economics with the support of his parents. He explained:

> I didn't feel like I was getting anywhere, and I was putting in the time and putting in the effort and my grades didn't reflect it, and my motivation was diminished because of it . . . [my parents] they weren't pushing me to stay in engineering, they were pushing me to stay in school, for me to do something I liked and wanted to do.

These two young men had been groomed, by their families, by the schools they attended, by the role models they had, to go to college and be successful. Having chosen engineering for basic economic reasons (good salary options and affluent life style), they found those reasons were not enough to keep them in a discipline where they perceived themselves misfits. The anxiety for these Black men was intensified because of the status of Black men in our society. J. R. summarized:

> Some people condemned me [for changing] because there is a lack of minority, a lack of African Americans in engineering, a lack of . . . you know, "Well there are so few of you there, you need to stick it out" and everything. And I'm like, "Well I'm not happy and I'm not doing well, It's not like I'm not happy and I'm doing excellent," you know. But I think they are also in correlation with each other. Granted that I'm satisfying a quota somewhere, putting another African American male in engineering, but there has to be some individual satisfaction in there too . . . individual, as an African American, I have to do something that's good for myself and not good for necessarily African American people by putting another face in engineering.

Reflections

In this study, I used open-ended questions such as "Tell me about your experience here in your freshman year" and obtained a variety of information about the things students had on their minds. For example Jay Jay remembered his freshman year:

> You're trying to center yourself but you're a freshman. You really don't know. So, I could have done a lot more but (pause) (I) was basically being a social butterfly freshman year. Concentrated on hanging out, going out and that, being a part of the group.

Johanna, not being a party person, remembered questioning her experience as being different:

> I think a lot of things affect you academically that you wouldn't really expect to affect you. Like I went through this before. In my freshman year my roommates were White and that affected me academically because it wasn't like I was out all night partying. But it was like the pressure of the world was on me. I'm like, "Why am I surrounded by Whiteness?" I mean, I really had a problem with that. It was like (my roommates) would go to bed at 11 o'clock. I'd be up studying and it was like, "Why do I have to study so

hard. Why? (pause) and then [them] getting the 4.0s and they're in bed. "Why is that?" ... It's not that "Oh, I'm Black, I'm stupid," or anything like that.

Tirae remembered the stigma of being singled out as the one who should need assistance:

I was the only Black student, and I was female. I remember my TA saying to me, "You know if you need any help, just let me know. Don't hesitate to call me." She was pacifying me. So I was just like, "Okay, I'm going to show this woman." I [thought] "You know maybe she is trying to be helpful—but at the same time she is really making me mad." ... I ended up getting an A in the course.

Stereotypes abound. These young women perceived their abilities were in question; that they, on the one hand, would have to work harder to do as well as White students. On the other hand, they felt they were suspect even before they had exhibited any ability. When asked "What stands out for you about your interactions with faculty?", Celeste's response summarized how these students expected to be treated in college and the value they placed on academic challenge:

There's a professor in (the) African American Studies Department, she is a very, very dominant Black woman. She has a lot of ideas that I might not necessarily agree with but I respect them because of the way that she presents them ... She expects quality and there's no way around it ... She pulled out a lot in me ... she made me work hard in her class. She made me analyze things in ways that I never really had to analyze them because of what she expected. And ... that has stayed with me in the way that I approach different kinds of books; in the way I approach different kinds of courses; that way she helped me analyze things. My analytical skills were definitely sharpened up in her class. It shows through my conversation.

These students are typical of Black students I have met on many campuses. They spoke candidly to me about their experiences—those that were painful and those that were strengthening.

To Be and *Not to Be*

Black students are expected *to be* and *not to be*. In order to be admitted to a private research university, Black students are expected to be at the top of their class in high school, expected to be average or above average in their SAT scores, and to be active in extracurricular activities. Black males are expected to be able to play basketball or football or both and run track but not to play soccer or lacrosse. If the Black students have these athletic talents (male or female), they are expected to be slow in their abilities in the classroom.

Conversely, Black students are not expected to be intelligent, critical thinkers; not expected to question the wisdom of university policies, procedures, or staff interpretations of these policies and procedures. They are not expected to be of upper- or upper middle-class background having had exposure to mainstream education, arts, and culture. It has been pointed out in an earlier chapter that this university, as well as other universities, recruit heavily in urban areas and in major cities from the larger, predominantly Black/ethnic high schools. It is not unreasonable to expect that university staff and students have stereotypical notions, vicariously imposed by the mass media, about the Black students who come from these urban areas.

To entice students to come to these universities, financial aid incentives are offered along with supportive services to ensure success. University brochures, program bulletins, and recruitment videos all represent the institution as having an environment conducive to learning and supportive of all students. In New York State there are several state programs and federally funded opportunities designed expressly for minority students who are "disadvantaged" educationally, economically, or socially, i.e., who are from a family with low socioeconomic status (SES). In order to qualify for these programs of financial aid and be able to attend a private research university, a student must qualify under one of these categories. It is a fact that significant numbers of Black students are from families that fit state and federal guidelines.

When Black students have the grades and scores to be regularly admitted, they may qualify for university scholarships. This scenario sets select Black students apart from the community of the other Black students in the sponsored programs. Suffice it to say, many Black students are caught in the middle—they need the camaraderie of other Black students but do not qualify for either the sponsored programs or the university scholarships. Many of the grant programs, and scholarship and fellowship programs include other designated underrepresented groups (Hispanic, Native American, women, etc.) as do those based on economics alone. I use only the category *Black* here because that group is the topic of my study. This is not meant to imply that any of these programs are exclusively for Blacks.

Supportive services programs were perceived by the Black students in this study to have a dual character: safe haven and stigma. Data in this study are replete with statements of the support and security students felt from the SI staff and the Minority Affairs Office staff: "Home away from home," "A place to breathe," "People who care about you," are just some of the phrases used to express the feelings associated with the programs housed "in the building on the other side of the Health Center." Students spoke of times when they needed assistance with other than academic issues, "They were there for me."

Students also talked about the resentment they felt at being labeled because they were Black, and at the negative connotations widely held by the university staff, faculty, and students. Kasey put it this way:

> . . . then the things that people think "Oh wow, you're getting a free ride," "You get financial aid," "The government's paying for this." But it's hard! It's like I said, I have two jobs. Plus I have my nineteen credits.

The impact of how widely, among students of color, this resentment was felt became clear to me during the viewing of the now classic *Frontline* program, *Racism 101* (1988). In the video, a White student, Michael Epstein, attempted to explain the stereotypical notions held by Whites:

> I think a lot of the underlying question in the White community is, Are the Blacks that come here as intelligent as I am? Are they able to perform as I am? . . . I think the reality though is, and I think that it's true for a lot of Whites who are probably unwilling to admit it—when a Black person makes as (sic) intelligent comment, there is a certain element of surprise. There is a certain element and this is very difficult to admit—there is a certain element that, this is not what I should—this is not what I should be getting from a Black person. (WGBH Educational Foundation, 1988)

This *Frontline* documentary, aired in 1988, drew strong reactions when shown to a group of students in a speech communication class on Syracuse University's campus in the 1994–1995 school year (Buttny, 1995). Students were asked to voluntarily tape their reactions to the video. In response to the perceptions of White students, one of three African American females in the group said:

> A lot of White students feel that if you're Black you are here because of a scholarship or affirmative action. I mean me and another White student talk about this, he says he can look around the room and pick which Blacks are here because of academics and which Blacks are here because of affirmative action by what they say in class and I was like you can't say that but you can say the same thing some of these White students here he was kind of like it's true for some of them but really it's mostly affected by Blacks, and every Black here is on a scholarship and I was like Hah, I'm not! You know that type of situation and that's how they feel that if you're Black and you're here at U it's because somebody gave you a handout and you don't really deserve it so you're beneath them and if you don't succeed it's your own fault and you were never really inclined to succeed, you were just here as a free ride, you know, and you're supposed to drop out.

A Black male student viewer put it this way:

> It's weird because I feel that the weight of the world is on my shoulders. I'm like damn I can't fail a class; I can't not do a report on time; I can't do bad on a test; you know it's like they look at me and go like (mimic a stereotypical White voice) "Gee them niggers they just must of gotten in on affirmative action or something like that you know."

The stigma is not caused by affirmative action or the supportive programs as much as by the stereotypical perceptions held by White students and staff, persons in positions with power over the progress of the students (e.g., faculty and financial aid officers), by members of other minority groups, and by the Black students themselves. Each student was constantly on guard against explicit and implicit hurtful interactions with people because of the color of their skin.

5

⚜ Students' Perceptions of Race

> An individual, Jay, is Black if Jay has one Black forebear, any number of generations back. An individual, Kay, is White if Kay has no Black forebears, any number of generations back.
>
> There is no other condition for racial Blackness that applies to every Black individual; there is no other condition for racial Whiteness that applies to every White individual.
>
> (Zack, 1993, p. 5)

Within the larger context of education and society in general, descriptive labels have been designated without consideration of the centuries of intermingling of races. By and large, Black students know their race and ethnicity; White students take for granted their Whiteness. The logic of Zack's representation, then, is inescapable because "Americans persist in using empirically unfounded racial designations" (1993). Since the 1960s, academia has become *racialized* as is indicated by racial designations in compliance with Civil Rights legislation, Equal Opportunity Programs, and Affirmative Action recruitment programs. In the 1980s standard categories were Caucasian, African American, Hispanic, American Indian, and Other. Currently, according to the U.S. Department of Education, the racial and ethnic designations used prior to 2000 were as follows: American Indian or Alaskan native; Asian or Pacific Islander; Black, non-Hispanic; Hispanic; White non-Hispanic; and Foreign. According to the American Council on Education, classifications indicating general racial or ethnic heritage are based on self-identification, as in data collected by the U.S. Census Bureau, or based on observational identification, as in data collected by agencies and/or scholars. These categories were in accordance with the Office of Management and Budget's standard classification scheme. There was also a category "race or ethnicity unknown," which was proportionally distributed across reported data (. . . Race makes a big difference, *Chronicle of Higher Education*, 1995). Financial aid and admissions applications list these racial categories as criteria for students to qualify for various fellowships, scholarships, and set-asides for members of groups underrepresented in certain disciplines. College students are subjected to self-selection criteria that in many ways may ignore part of students' natural heritage.

According to Jacqueline Jordan Irvine (1991), on the one hand, the purpose of education is believed to be positively and directly related to productivity, for both the individual and the society, and to economic development. This position is illustrated by such egalitarian goals as preparation of the work force for the twenty-first century or an increase in the number of qualified "minorities" in technical fields. Conversely, there is a strong belief that "the power of the dominant social group determines economic and educational requirements and that the interest of the powerful is principally to maintain and replicate the status quo, which results in a system of inequality for others." (Irvine, 1991 p.2). Graduation rates nationally for all students are indicative of this second position. Diverse students are being recruited, but graduation rates for all but Asian students lag dismally behind those of White students. Still today, underrepresented students are traditionally expected to assimilate and learn from within an environment largely unfamiliar with and unaccepting of them and their culture.

Students in this study spoke about the racism on campus in the 1990s in the same terms as the students in a similar study conducted by Willie & McCord (1972) more than three decades ago among four campuses in the Syracuse, New York area. At that time racial incidents were overt. Many in society believed that if Black students wanted higher education, they should go to the Black colleges and universities that had been set up specifically for them. While the Civil Rights Movement had changed the laws, attitudes were not so easily legislated. Change came slowly.

Kasey, a participant in this study, was aware of some of these attitudes. She recalled her feelings during a Political Science class discussion about drugs and drug trafficking:

> It's just that I'm very aware of the things that can happen. I don't limit our government on anything—especially from my background in that—in the kind of laws that were passed, that told me that I was nobody and that I was 3/5 of somebody and 2/3 of somebody, know what I'm saying... It used to be like, "Wow! These people are really unaware that, when I'm home, somebody's getting shot or something every two or three hours maybe, if it's a good weekend." But it's like, being that they are not aware of where I come from and how I live and the way I was brought up, they may not understand my reactions to certain things. Like we had a flag burning this year and I was like, "burn it; I don't care," and people were like "Well, go back to where you came from." And I was like, "Well, first of all". . . you have to be careful. You have to be very careful how you term things and how you say it to people.

Kasey's "burn it" came from an attitude held by many Black students who are being treated as if they were not Americans entitled to equal citizenship with other Americans.

On one level, Black students believed that if accepted to a predominantly White institution, they would be able to get a better education because predominantly White institutions have more resources and better reputations than historically Black colleges and universities. It was Tirae who commented on students' attitudes and her own:

> I think a lot of students are into that mentality "I go to college to get a job." . . . My whole thing is the first thing you have a degree in is being Black. There is a whole art to being Black. It is a strange sort of way, but Black people all over the world say you can't escape the racism, you can't escape any of the _isms, really.

At yet another level, Black students today talk about missing something by not going to a historically Black college or university, not being able to *"feel like you belong."* One student, Yoclee, was clear about which type of college she wanted to go to. Being offered scholarship aid made the big difference. Here is how she told it:

> So I applied to all the Black colleges. I applied to Hampton. I applied to Spelman. I applied to North Carolina Central University, and none of them accepted me. None of the African American colleges accepted me, and SU did accept me. SU accepted me. Binghamton accepted me. A lot of the upstate schools accepted me. Syracuse White universities accepted me! . . . Syracuse is a more prestigious college. I talked to my guidance counselor and so he said, "Good. Go to Syracuse." And they said they were going to accept me in the HEOP program.

It is not clear why Yoclee was not accepted by the predominantly Black schools. Yet, there may be underlying necessities in the form of reasons why Syracuse University and other upstate White schools did accept her—quotas, representation, diversity, image. Yoclee said her choice of Syracuse was "a joke" and added, "to me, I summarized that there is a reason for me being here." Yoclee figured it was by divine plan.

Perception of Difference

> Racism is a slippery subject, one which evades confrontation, yet one which overshadows every aspect of our lives. And because so few (White) people are directly and honestly talking about it, we . . . have once again had to take on the task. Making others 'uncomfortable' in their Racism is one way of 'encouraging' them to take a stance against it. (Anzaldúa, 1990)

In the 1980s and 1990s, the "incongruity of expectations," as posited by Jacqueline Fleming (1984), was muted by the rhetoric of recruitment and support on the part of institutions and the prevailing perception on the part of Black students that the White institution was the better institution. In reality, Black students at a predominantly White institution have a *Black Experience* resulting from what was once termed an "incompatibility of expectations." Jewel T. Gibbs, in her 1973 study, discussed this incompatibility of expectations of both the university and the Black students. I briefly enumerate her findings here to show their similarity to the concerns of students in the current study. According to Gibbs's study, university expectations were that Black students would:

- naturally assimilate without benefit of special programs or staff;
- have similar academic preparation and skills as White students;
- get involved in sociocultural life of the campus, and not seek their own cultural and ethnic campus life;
- be grateful for being able to come to the institution.

Black students, in contrast, expected that the university would:

- help Black students get through bureaucracy by bending rules and giving unconditional financial aid;
- have course work at the level where students were in high school;
- offer the ethnic and cultural activities students were used to;
- have open, cordial relations with the Black community surrounding the campus and be aware of services students need i.e., barber and beauty salons, churches, [ethnic] foods;
- expect and accept the students' contributions to the campus community. (Gibbs, 1973)

Based on data from the present study, there is still an incongruence of expectations held by the university and the Black students.

Even though the phrase "Black Experience" was coined in the 1970s, students told me about their *Black Experience* as they reviewed their *pre-college* campus experience (for those who attended), and their freshman, sophomore, junior, and senior years and, for some, the additional time they spent as students on a predominantly White university campus. My data indicate that these Black and African American students have had many experiences in common, for many reasons—because of the SI program, because of their *culture, ethnicity, and race*, and because of their daily interactions being Black on a White campus.

Before proceeding, let me clarify the three terms in the previous statement that are often used synonymously: culture, ethnicity, and race. Elaine Pinderhughes (1989), a professor of psychology, submits that these terms are distinct and describes each, as follows: "*Culture* is viewed as the sum total of ways of living that a group of human beings develops to meet biological and psychological needs" (p. 6). It refers, for example, to values, norms, beliefs, attitudes, folkways, behavior styles, and traditions. These elements function together to preserve the society. "*Ethnicity* refers to connectedness based on commonalities" such as religion, nationality, region, etc. (p. 6). Cultural patterns are shared and transmission over time creates a common history. Pinderhughes (1989) adds: "*Race*, while a biological term, takes on ethnic meaning when and if members of that biological group have evolved specific ways of living." As it is applicable to the interaction on a college campus, "*Race* takes on a cultural significance as a result of the social processes that sustain majority-minority status" (p. 9).

The continuation of Pinderhughes's quote is relevant to the discussion of Black/White social interaction in a much broader, societal context. I include it here as a note on the discussion at hand. She continues:

> (1) The subordinate status assigned to persons with given physical (racial) traits and the projections made upon them are used to justify exclusion or inclusion within society; in this sense race takes on the meaning of caste; (2) the responses of both those who are dominant, and therefore exclude, and the victims who are subordinate, and therefore excluded, become part of their cultural adaptation. The meaning assigned to class status as well as racial categorization is determined by the dynamics of stratification and to some degree stereotyping. (p. 9)

It was the different stereotypes of "African Americans" held by students, faculty, administrators, and staff members at the university and the resulting treatment that Black students in this study talked about as "the stuff—acts of racism, prejudice, discrimination—you have to deal with every day."

Common Experiences and Differing Perspectives

While it is true that these Black and African American students had common experiences on this predominantly White campus, these students' experiences and perspectives also differed, according to their socioeconomic status and family educational backgrounds. Students in this study talked candidly about what it was like to be singled out, put on the spot, and not included. They talked about formal student groups, sororities, fraternities, and the informal cliques and groups where they found comfort.

Jay Jay talked about how students make choices. He believed:

> Basically, it's a part of your environment. It's a part of your culture. And I do believe this firmly, that the way you are raised, who you are raised with, defines your mentality; defines your (pause) your ideas and your beliefs. Not color. [Jay is Biracial and could "pass" for White.] Some people ask me why I didn't join a White fraternity, why did I join a Black fraternity? Because, they had more of the things that I believe in. So, I believe in an African American community. So I will support that. And there are just certain things you feel at ease with. Like African Americans who join a White fraternity, they join it because that's who they hung around with, that's who they feel comfortable with.

Johanna is Black, but not American. Her perspective was a broader one given the fact that she had only been in America approximately five years, since her second year in high school. She considered herself well grounded enough in her identity so as not to be concerned about how people categorized her. She commented:

> I think about it [being perceived as an African American], . . . I am a Black woman. I mean, I don't get offended if people call me African American at all because, you know, to me it's just another term for Black. [The fact of not

being African American] affects a lot—I think I feel other things differently and more universally. I think, especially since my parents are West Indian, but I wasn't born in the West Indies or raised in the West Indies. I was born in England, so I just had all these different perspectives on a lot of things.

Rema, a Black student born in Haiti, reared in Brooklyn, New York, made a point that just because other people think of you as a "minority" does not mean that you think of yourself that way. Her comment was:

> ... when you were here [during the Summer Institute] the people were not the people who were here when you came back. When we came back, we were like, "Oh, so this is what it's like to be a minority." It was like, "Where are we?" When we saw somebody from Summer Institute across the quad it was like "Oh!" It was so amazing that there were a lot, a lot of White people.

She explained her perspective:

> I went to a bilingual school where I was from elementary to high school. Bilingual: French-English and Spanish-English. So I was always basically with my people. So when I came here over the summer, it was the same thing, pretty integrated. When I came here [in the fall] it was like, "Oh!" "So this is what it is really like."

Maria's perspective was:

> I find that, although this is a predominantly European American university, you still, as an African American ... I feel as though I'm still in my own type of world as far as African Americans are concerned. I mean, I interact with the European Americans only when I'm in class, but outside of class we go our separate ways. And sometimes I feel like the university is segregated in that sense. We go our own separate ways and I don't feel ... sort of alienated.

In addition to the differences in backgrounds and ethnic combinations, these students came from different parts of the country and different types of locations: rural, urban, suburban. Rema was from the "City" and Maria was from a rural town. Yoclee spoke about these differences:

> I know many of [the other Black students], and I know that we have—the ones that I have come in contact with—we have different views about different things. I guess because of our back—our different backgrounds.

These realities surfaced as issues which students have to deal with every day. Yoclee continued:

> For example how—we can use things, like how we cook, some of the things that we eat. Living in a projects [in lower Manhattan]; we're used to going down to the corner store where there is a Chinese restaurant and buy food instead of cooking. Whereas, she [another Black woman] had come from a home where there was etiquette, for example where people—they sat at the table and ate. And they kept their elbows off the table and they—you know. Things like that, where we get a piece of chicken, put it in our hands and go to town. (laughter) You know and she sits. She cuts her chicken with knives and—and it was a problem for her because—she sort of labeled us savages or something.

It was these cultural differences among the African American students on campus, the subtle and not so subtle racism, along with their choices of friends and organizations that surfaced as problematic for these students.

Subtle and Not So Subtle

The racism was a *daily* occurrence mentioned by most students. Maria shared a very personal travesty:

> That was in freshman year. And in freshman year I dated an Italian from Brooklyn, and you know, we were just friends. I didn't realize. You know. We had friends that were everyone, and one day he came to me and said, "I can't date you any more. I know it's terrible of me, but my family would disown me. They would cut me off from millions and billions of dollars if they even knew." That was a whole new concept. He said, "I really care about you. But I like you a lot. But I can't be with you because, you know. My mom doesn't even want me to speak to an African American woman, and if she knew you and I were going out, and kissing, and you know. I would be cut off from the family money." I thought, "What is this?" Maybe it was just the experience that I had. But, then I realized it's very important as an identity.

Identity and How It Gets Sorted Out . . .

Maria, the third student I interviewed, was the first student to use the word identity. However, identity, and how it gets sorted out, became one of the major themes all students mentioned as part of their experience on this predominantly White campus. Maria experienced turmoil because of being Biracial and being from a small town, as well as not being in any special programs. She lived all four years on main campus, but freshman year was the worst as she told it:

> But still, I wasn't on south campus, and that right there excludes you a little. I tried to get into NAACP as a freshman and I felt that people there thought, "Why is she here?" I don't know. I don't know what it was, but I attribute a lot of it to just me being Black, or not Black enough, or not White enough or whatever. I just didn't know where to fit in. I took a course in African American history. I loved it so much that I said "I want to do something with this." And [fourth semester] I made it my major. I noticed when I started having classes with a lot of African Americans, the same people that had seen me for years turned their heads and didn't say "Hello" when I said "Hello." All of a sudden, "Oh, that's why you were in my last semester courses. Well, what's your major?" Or, even just . . . People who didn't see me in a class but saw me on campus were forced to talk to me for whatever reason. We came into contact somewhere. "Oh, what's your major?" "African American Studies." "Oh!" and then there was this welcoming all of a sudden. And it was all such a phony that I saw. It took me a long time to understand.

Yoclee's earlier statement described struggles where identity was based on region and perceived SES as an African American. Similar identity concerns developed for the Black women in regards to the choices of whether or not to join Black sororities (see Giddings, 1998). Maria's, Jay Jay's and Randi's identity search had more to do with their Biracial beginnings and value choices. These students had the opportunity to learn about the values and mores of two or more cultures from childhood and thus had multiple frames of reference to choose from. Johanna's and Rema's choices of friends and socialization were similar based on their broader view of the world and having family from England and the Caribbean. Not all Black students have a multicultural frame of reference.

Students' identities evolved as they became involved in student organizations and professional majors on campus. The "belonging" with other students buffeted the daily assaults to the students' personal dignity that they experienced in interactions with people on campus. Freddie began his socializing like most college freshmen:

> Well, socially a lot of my social relationships came out of the activities that I was involved in. I think that first year I may have attended more parties than I would attend in the next two years of my college career. I think that Syracuse University is a school which has a very good social environment.

Freddie included the formal student organization structure in his description of the social environment at Syracuse University. Having been a very active student leader, this is what he had to say about the Black organizations on campus:

> Many African American students come into the university seeking a better understanding of their own background and a better understanding of themselves as they wish to be . . . so that African American Studies—which came out of the efforts of S.A.S. 25 years ago—becomes an important institution and worked sort of hand-to-hand with some of the efforts that the Student African American Society put forth. So I think that an institution such as S.A.S. allows for autonomy, and it gives students the opportunity to have an environment where they can speak freely about their experiences and share ideas as African Americans and, in an environment which is non-hostile. Whereas often in a general university setting or even in many of our classrooms African Americans are only representative of approximately 10% of the student population. Often we are well outnumbered in our classroom settings and many of us are hesitant to express our views because our views, for many of us, clash with the Eurocentric [views] in a sense that all things take sides. . . . meeting others allows for students to sharpen their intellectual skills or what have you and [S.A.S.] actually provides an academic arm to the university. And in that way it is helping to sharpen the intellectual tools of students who are then better able to go into the classroom and perform at their peak. So, in so many ways I think institutions such as S.A.S. and BCCE (Black Celestial Choral Ensemble) on the other hand are important in the retention of African American students.

Tirae, from a different perspective, used a video game as an interesting metaphor for the life of a Black student on a predominantly White campus:

> It is like culture shock every day. You are used to it, but it is culture shock every day. You live in your room and everything in there represents you, or it should represent you. That represents me [she refers to a fabric map of Africa on her wall], everything in there. Then I walk outside and it is a whole different story. It is kind of like being on a video game. Because you are walking outside and you see all of these things and you are ducking and dodging this and you are ducking and dodging that, and you are trying to avoid this stuff going on over here in the corner. So your only outlet becomes what you do in your spare time.

She sums it up:

> But that is the way it is. It is rough. People get stressed. I am talking about stress just BEING, on this campus, just dealing with the every day nonsense. It is actually—so common that you actually forget things like the racism every day. The people. You know . . . You just get so tired of it day in and day out. It wears on you.

The cohort of students interviewed had formed lasting friendships during the precollege SI program, among the Black choir, as members of "minority" student groups, or among community families and churches. Support groups as *safe havens* formed in the first two or three semesters, grew more important as the years continued. Social activities, such as dances, cultural gatherings sponsored by Black organizations, membership and participation in groups, and working with the "community service projects," were important aspects of each of these students' experience on campus.

Consequently, these interactions with friends, different living arrangements (locations and roommates), as well as "what's acceptable or not acceptable" socializing to African American students (race and interracial dating, where to hang out, drinking, segregation), reflected how students "were able to handle everything else" about being Black on this predominantly White campus. Several students related lengthy critical incidents from classroom experience or with faculty. There was a mixture of remarks, positive and not so positive: "The faculty don't really interact with you" or "Anyway, they think we can't do the work" or "We always have to work harder."

The overwhelming number of "majority" students was a "culture shock" to most African American students coming back in the fall after the SI program. Subtle but constant racism was the condition that these students most resented. All of the students interviewed mentioned racism and having been affected by it either in a classroom, an administrative office, or an incident with students on campus. Racism is a major theme running through all of the students' years at the university.

6

✣ Talk About Being Visible and Invisible

The following are incidents in the experience of three of the Black students in my study which, according to the students, were the kinds of situations that happen because of "ignorance," racism, and the way White people regard Black people. These accounts are in the students' own words as transcribed from their interviews. My clarifying questions are indicated.

Dano's Experience with Security—Fall 1989
DANO: Basically, I went and made an appointment with Eunice (the Director) about signing up with Minority Affairs Office, and I came back the day of the appointment and I got to the appointment, I guess, a little early and I walked into the building and I see a guy standing at the window. Later I found out he was a security officer and [he was wearing] plain clothes. And he's looking at me and I guess you know, it's relatively still early in the year, early in the semester, and so, you know, I didn't really want to pay him any attention and I go to the elevator and I see him coming up behind me like through the view of the elevator glass, and so I take the steps. I take the steps to the third floor and I see him coming to the steps. I say (to myself), "why is this guy...." But I didn't even think, didn't know this campus. You don't mind anything... I said "Why is this guy following me?" So I sit down and I check in with the receptionist. Eunice, as I was checking in with the receptionist, came out and said, "I'll be right back." She has to run down the hall and she said she'd be right back. So I'll just wait. She said "Wait." So OK, fine. So I'm

sitting there waiting and he comes up to me and says, "Where is your . . . Can I see your ID or some form of identification." I'm like, "Excuse me, what are you asking me for?" [He said] "I want to see some ID or identification." I said "Who are you?"

He pulls out a badge. It's a badge. No identification on the badge. It's not like a badge a police officer would show you with an ID on top and the badge on the bottom. He just pulls out a badge. So then I asked him what right do you have—who are you and what right do you have to ask me any questions? And he's like "This is my right as an officer." I'm like, "I don't know what that is. I don't know if that's real or what. That's just a badge to me. That means nothing to me. I'm not going to show you anything." So then we got into an argument. I said "Why don't you show me some ID?" And he got offended because I challenged him from this point. And I really didn't have any ID on me because I had just come from . . . I don't know what, I was playing a game of softball or something and I had sweats on. And with sweats, you know those popular sweats with the drawstring. I didn't have any pockets, so I just sort of grabbed a bag. You know how when you're just coming from class, kind of walking. I wasn't even planning on playing softball, you just walking back and forth, you know you meet a lot of people. Went back, sitting and I'm like . . . but I didn't even remember that . . . I didn't have the ID with me. So I'm like, "Who are you anyway?"

And the receptionist is just sitting there. I'm like, well, shouldn't she say something? Being this is the Minority Affairs Office and she saw Eunice come out and talk to me, shouldn't she say something, like, "What are you doing?" And she didn't say anything. You know, it's like, "That's it, forget it, this is stupid, I'm leaving." And he says, "You're not going anywhere." "What do you mean I'm not going anywhere? Hey, wait a minute." And he calls, like "I'm going to need backup. And then like three more security officers come up. I'm like "Wait! Wait! Who the hell are these guys?" There's a big . . . I'm arguing like "You guys . . . I don't give a damn who you are!"; big arguing match . . . getting loud, people are coming out and looking at the officers. I'm making a scene here. Eunice comes. She's like

"What's going on?" And she found out. She wasn't pleased because here's a student sitting in her office and it's a Minority Services Office, what do you expect to see there? And he gives a description and what pissed me off, we had one of the other officers says "We had a description of a . . . And they gave you a description . . . the guy was supposed to be. I remember I was weighing 160 something at the time . . . the guy they had was like 210 (lbs), over 6 (ft) . . . I'm not sure how tall I was . . . I was just getting on 6 ft . . . the guy they had was 6'3", 6'4", lightly shaven. I still don't shave. To this day, I still don't shave. This guy had a light beard. I mean this is just a general description of any Black [male] person. You know, I realize that, and I realized that right on the spot. This is just a general . . . this gives you the right to pullover any . . . "six foot with a little Afro, short on the sides." Because I was wearing a Fade, when this came about. [A Fade was the name of the particular haircut fashion of the day for Black males.] Everybody had a Fade. This is ridiculous . . . this is every Black on campus. I remember telling him, "Why don't you pull in the basketball team or go harass the football team?" Don't bother me." To me that was every single Black guy over 6', between 6' and 6'4". That's a lot, you know, that's easy.

I asked if they told him why they were looking for this person.

They told Eunice that [why they were looking for this person] . . . no they didn't tell me, they never told me . . . they told Eunice. Then I got mad, because when they realized they were wrong, they tried to talk me into another office because I remember saying "Why don't you let me speak to your boss." I remember I was really going off. Then somebody else came up and they took me to another office; they wanted to talk to me. And then they offered me a job working for security. So, I just did not understand. I remember the guy saying "Well I don't think you understand how tough our job is. Maybe you'd like to come work for us." I said, "You're joking. You're not offering me a job." He said "I think you'd understand if you worked for us." I said "No, no, no. No way in hell do I want to work with you guys." [We laughed] And because I was involved with S.A.S., I found out that this happens to a lot of students, a lot of Black students.

This happens to a number of Black students on this campus, using that same description. For a while, if you walked into the Security Office you'd see that description. Yes, [this was in] '88, '89. So, it happened to a couple of folks, and just because I was in S.A.S. I noticed. I'm sure . . . I don't think it's as bad now. Security has a . . . I don't know if it's as bad . . . Security stopped after the protests. It was pointing out that Black students were being harassed, Black males from here. Then I realize now and that Security has become pretty good at it too, being able to identify Black students from Black people who live in Syracuse. And they can identify 'em, because I now I can tell. You can tell; I don't know why. Especially like at dances or anything, you can just tell. Security has become good at that; but they can still be wrong. They're just like any Black student, which is bad and good . . . because it still happens.

Eunice was very displeased, but, I mean, she's a professional. She wasn't going to get upset like me. If it happened to me now, I wouldn't get upset. You know what I mean. But at that time, you just get upset. You're not used to these things happening to you. You're just sick of it. She said something to me, like people tend to bring things with them. I hadn't. I didn't like mine, because mine was rather racially motivated. It's that type of town. Not that New York isn't, but mine you know, I don't know how to explain the difference.

Blacks do have some sort of power base in New York, and I came here and I did not expect it and it caught me and I was like, "Wait a minute, not here, you're not going to do that here. You're not going to harass me." I think it was a good experience in the sense that it kind of snapped me to reality. You just really need to stay in the organizations and you need to . . . you can't afford to relax and say, "Oh, it's okay." I never forgot that experience. I think everything happens for a reason.

Tirae on Classroom Experience

TIRAE: It is kind of funny because when I look back after I graduate and I look back on Syracuse, I won't remember the work. I will remember everything else that happened . . . You do what you have to do, you go to your classes. You take little notes that don't make any sense anyway. The teacher wrote the book, and the book is 50 years outdated. But you do it anyway. After that, it is what you make it. It is all about, let me go run down to the S.A.S. office and see who is in there just so I can sit and talk to somebody to keep my peace of mind. That is what it is about and that is why [someone] said that college is an experience in itself, but I am more concerned with talking to individuals who are trying to help people, with doing what I do in the organizations than I am about school work. That doesn't mean that I don't care. It just means that, obviously it is not worth the money you are paying for it, for one thing. But another thing is that something needs to change. I shouldn't go through four years of college and not remember my classes and things like that. But that is the way it is. It is rough. People get stressed. I am talking about stress just BEING on this campus, just dealing with the everyday nonsense. It is actually so, what is the word I am looking for? So common that you actually forget things like the racism every day. The people, you know, the girl sitting next to you in class and you go to ask her a question, and she turns her head as if she doesn't see you. And the professor that doesn't want to call on you, even though there are only two people with their hands up and things like that. You just get so tired of it day in and day out. It wears on you.

What was it like in class when you were asked to be participative, or were you?

Right. And I am still doing in class things like the Greeks and the Romans contribute everything to the New World, so to speak. And you know it is not true. You raise your hand and say, "Okay, well what about, you know, what the Africans contribute?" And so on and so forth. They say, "Well, you know, that really hasn't been proven."

Then the teacher goes on to the next subject. That is so common. If you stand there and try and tell the teacher. Well, you sit there and argue your point, then it is all about, "Why are you making this a race thing?" It is never a race thing for White people, it is always a race thing for Black people. I remember one class, WSP (Women Studies) 101, Introduction to language, culture and something . . . . It was an introductory class, and I didn't know anything about feminism, so I was like okay, it was an introduction to feminism class. I was like, okay, well, along those lines. So I said, let me take this class. I had been trying to take it since freshman year, but it was always closed out. So I finally got it junior year, and I was like, "Good." So I got into the class and we had a lot of different folks. We had a book with a whole bunch of articles and things in it. We had a book from a Nigerian author, which is a very good book. We had a book, what is the name of that book? It was Yellow Walls Or Yellow Wallpaper, it was a very thin book, something. So we began our course work, and in the book it had a lot of different articles, there was an article, "Angela Davis on Reproductive Rights." She was talking about sterilization and how this should be illegal because the government only, oftentimes they try to get Black women to agree to sterilization and so on and so forth. Well, in the course, all through the course the professor kept telling us, we don't have a lot of time, I am trying to cram everything in. We had to read this book about these yellow walls, and it was about this White woman who was married to this man, and he wouldn't let her do anything. Basically, the husband controls her. She ended up going crazy. I was making the difference, the point being that I am not saying that there aren't any Black women like that, but that oftentimes, you know the Black women are kind of like, "Okay, I'm glad you feel that way but I still have to do what I have to do." And it was funny because no one, it was myself and two other Black students and the rest were students who were White . . . White females, and the rest of the students were White. The men who were in the class were very quiet. They didn't say anything, but they were White males. No one understood that. So here I am, I'm mad because there is only a couple of us in there, and we have to defend the whole Black race. I have to explain everything to them, and I'm like, "Doggone it!" I was so mad because they don't know anything about us. Therefore, I have to sit down and start from square one just to get to my points, to say, you know, it is the point . . . Anyway, she was always saying how we didn't have a lot of materials, we didn't have enough time, rather. So, it was time to read this article, and this was a great article. It was like, "I can't wait to discuss this. I am so psyched." I walked into class that day and she said, we will not be discussing this because we don't have enough time; therefore, read such and such. Well, my hand went up I don't know how fast. By this time, I was being rude and indignant because I was really sick of this hypocrisy. I said, "Look, let me tell you something. Whether you want to discuss this or not" . . . and I said it with an attitude, and I meant it. I said, "We are discussing Angela Davis in the next class." I said, "How dare you tell us we don't have enough time, but yet we can read that little stupid book you gave us about that White woman who didn't have enough guts to stand up to her husband." Now this is what I told her. And the whole class was like, she is a _____. They thought I was crazy. I said . . . "And another thing," and by this time I had brought up the fact in class that we did not discuss Black feminism and I was upset about that. I told her and the TA that if you do not know about Black feminism, you need to get someone in here to tell us about it. I said, "I don't know anything about feminism." I know now that feminism is very White, which is why there is a need for Black feminism. I said, "Now, I can't tell you everything about Black feminism, because I don't really know anything. So if you don't know anything, you need to get someone in here who can tell me, or you need to go back to school, which I do suggest." So by this time, I am just out of control. I am just going off in class. You know. All my points are valid, and by this time, the whole class has labeled me a bitch, because I just have to say what I have to say. So, she looked at me, and she said, "Okay, we will discuss Angela Davis the next time in class." So, the next class came around, and I knew she was going to want me to start the discussion. She wasn't a very aggressive teacher, which she could say, "Let's call on . . .," "Who wants to say . . . whatever?" Or if no one had anything to say, she wouldn't discuss it. She would just go on to something else, and she wasn't aggressive enough to say, "Okay, let's talk about such and such." I knew she was going to wait for me to start the discussion. We sat in that class for probably two (2) minutes with no one saying anything. Everyone staring at me waiting for me to start the Angela Davis discussion. I raised my hand. And when I raised my hand everyone sighed. But they didn't know what I was going to say. I raised my hand and I said, "I know you are waiting for me to start the discussion, but I refuse to." Then the tension level went back up again. They were like, "Damn, she is really a bitch." So I was sitting there and I refused to say something. So she started it, which she should have done anyway since she is the professor. Another thing I pointed out to her. . . about the difference between Black women and White women. I had to let her know there is a difference. I'm a student, I don't know anything about this, I'm running your class. "Get a grip!" So anyway, it was so funny now that I think about it. We ended up discussing it, and it was a really good discussion. I said to her, "You were going to skip this much and look what happened! We talked about a million other things from it." I also met with her outside of class, and I told her that I thought her class needed to be revamped because it did not include Black feminists, and if she didn't know it, she should call someone in here. She said, "Well, I think people would get offended." I said, "No, if that is their special interest, they are not studying it to get offended. They are studying it so they can tell other people about it." I said, "Therefore, you need to find someone that can speak about it and bring them to your classroom. You don't know, or you need to go take a class with them and come back and tell it right."

Violet's Experience with Engineering, Financial Aid, Supportive Services, and Arts and Sciences

VIOLET: Well, it was 1988. That's when I graduated from high school and I had narrowed down my choices between Notre Dame and Syracuse University. I was interested in attending a Black university.

At the time I was involved in aerospace engineering, but there was not a single Black university in the United States that offered aerospace engineering. I also figured it would be good to go to a predominantly White university so that I would get used to dealing with that environment, you know, being one of the few in the crowd, I guess you could say. So I chose Syracuse because I am from Cincinnati, Ohio, and I figured that this is far enough away so I can learn to be independent and be me, instead of somebody else's daughter or granddaughter, because both sets of my family are from Cincinnati. So, you go through your little freshman orientation programs after I got dropped off and I looked around and I was the only Black female entering the freshman class in engineering. And I was really scared, because I figured I would probably be one of five or one of three, but I didn't figure I would be the only one, and, um, there must have been about 15 Black students total. . . . So there were about 22 of us total. Six of us are female. We have the first floor. It was good because that way whenever I had trouble with my homework, I had someone else to help me out. And fortunately there was another Black student . . .two of us . . .one male, one female . . .I guess they filled their quota. And his name was Brian and he introduced me to the National Society of Black Engineers (NSBE) and that really helped me out a lot because then I didn't feel so isolated. Because I went to my classes and everything and I was still very conscious of being the only one, so to speak, and because early in your freshman year, they differentiate according to major, like aerospace mechanical and civil and then they have like electrical doing whatever they have to do . . . There was one other Black male who was in mechanical. He ended up leaving engineering before I did. So by the end of the freshman year he was completely out, and I was back to being lonely again. With the National Society of Black Engineers, they have this big brother and sister program, and it was so sad because the only two people who could be my big brother or big sister was one male and one female. They were both aerospace engineer majors, and they were both seniors, so I was really thinking to myself . . . gee, I'm going to be here by myself another year. But I persevered . . . I enjoyed it because I was geared towards the math and sciences already. I already knew what I wanted to do since the age of 12. So, you know, during high school I took calculus, physics, all that other kind of stuff, so I would be halfway prepared, not completely. And to make a nice long story short, I ended up being named the Freshman of the Year in the National Society of Black Engineers, this chapter. So I was very happy and very touched . . . and I went home, my parents patted me on the back. The only problem was I was used to achieving and getting a 3.0 to a 3.5 GPA in high school and I went from that to getting a 2.3. But, part of that was getting used to the new environment and everything, a very difficult course load because they throw 16 credits at you per semester immediately and that's chemistry, calculus . . .

As a freshman?

Freshman, yes. They make it quite clear to you that within the first two years, they're going to weed you out, and my grandmother passed away the second semester, so that was difficult for me. We were very close . . .

Second semester of your freshman year?

Of my freshman year, right. So 2.3 cum was pretty good, I think. I came back and I just knew I was going to do better because I am somewhat of a perfectionist, so to speak. So, it's the sophomore year now, it's the fall of 1989. I got sick. I had mono and if I didn't have mono, I had strep, and if I didn't have strep, I had mono. So this is for the whole year, and this is when . . . you know your sophomore year . . . that's when classes really get specialized. . . . Your first year, they give you your basic calculus, your basic physics. Your sophomore year in aerospace, they give you statistics and dynamics, and the lab on computer courses and things like that. There is very little time to take regular liberal arts courses, like African American Studies, but I always made the point or when I had time in my schedule, I was going to take an African American Studies class partly because I had not learned a lot about that in high school and I ended up taking one or two in my freshman year and that turned me on. It really helped out with my engineering courses.

How's that?

Because with my engineering courses, you know how there is the saying where people gravitate towards different career choices depending upon their personality. With engineering, it is very mechanical, very analytical. You just come in your class . . . you usually have a male first of all as a professor and he's also going to be a White male. He's up in front of the classroom . . . big lecture hall or big classroom . . . about 50 people . . . and there is very little exchange between teacher and student. And me, once again, being the only Black female that made it even harder for me. Also . . . yeah, that's just another story that I just remembered. I had this one professor for my first aerospace engineering class, first semester, sophomore year . . . he was passing back exams. I had not been to see the TA or him yet. He looked at my exam and said "(My last name)" . . . he looked right at me . . . he gave me my exam. So he already knew who I was. And that just really turned me out. Because, I haven't even been to see these people yet but they know who I am. Why do they know who I am? Also, observations in classes that there was definite discrimination between females and non-White students in class. If you raised your hand, you would be the last person to be called upon or they would interrupt whatever you had to say. Whereas, as you know, you had your White male students who could go on and on and have almost soliloquies and teach their own class, so to speak. So my GPA went down really badly in my sophomore year and I ended up going from a 2.3 to a 1.5 cum. That was class upon class upon class, and since I am a perfectionist, I was very hardheaded . . . I didn't want to go home. I was just like, no, I am not going to do this. I had something to prove to myself because I felt that I also had something to prove to other people. The people who were in my class, the people who were my professors, also my parents. Part of the other problem was . . . my parents are divorced . . .my mother is in Cincinnati . . . my father is in California. My father has never been particularly crazy about me becoming an engineer because as he said there is not very good marketing for that unless it was civil or electrical. And I explained to him that there was no way on the planet Earth that I was going to be a civil because I don't care about sewage systems and I was not going to be electrical. So then I was also having difficulty with my mother because, you know, there is a period of adjustment that takes place with your child when they go away to school and they come back the first time and they just know they're grown . . . so they're used to doing things their way now and you're used to them doing things that they used to do a certain way. So that was a very, very difficult summer, especially trying to tell my parents about what happened with classes, grades, and everything. I let them know that I was sick, but I didn't let them know that I was doing so poorly because that really hurt my self-image and my pride. My father ended up finding out anyway because Syracuse University decided that I no longer needed to be here . . . not part-time, not full-time, nothing. It's bad enough that engineering was kicking me out, but the university too.

Was there anyone who talked to you about that first?

No, I got a little letter in the mail, and somebody should have spoken to me about it because for one, seeing that I was an active member of the National Society of Black Engineers, we have an advisor. I didn't hear a word from him. It's partly his department. I need to hear from him if I'm not hearing from anybody else. Point number two, I did not hear from anybody in the College of Engineering until middle July, and you know we get out of school in the beginning of May. Now, I knew something was coming, but I wasn't exactly sure what. People were very hard to get in touch with. I called and I called and I wasn't getting my phone calls returned. As a matter of fact, with financial aid, one particular counselor, she finally got in touch with her—say in August—and you know school starts up in a couple more weeks.

And this is someone in the Financial Aid Office?

She calls me back finally after I have called and called and called and run up the phone bill and everything, two, three days before it's time to come back to school. And she tells me that I need to set up these petitions and all this other kind of thing so that I can get back into the university at the very least as a part-time student. I'm like, "Okay, fine." So I write all my little letters, send them out and everything and I come back up to campus anyway. That was against both my parents' wishes—my father's because my GPA was so low— and I had gotten kicked out of engineering and I had neglected to tell him that, he was like, "You're not getting any money from me." My mother... she really wasn't giving me money either, partly because of our difficulties, and also because she's a school teacher. So, if you have a school teacher on one side trying to support two kids on her own with a part-time job, and you have your father who is the budget director of Veinus County, there is a little bit of difference in income here. So, I did come back here . . .everything was okay as far as getting housing and my meal plan and everything. I had about roughly a month to take care of all that business before they were going to kick me out completely. So, I did a lot of running around my own self because no one pointed me out in any directions... you know, that I needed to go speak with Student Support Services, or I need to go speak directly to the director of financial aid, and on, and on, and on. So I did end up wheedling my way back into semi-good graces for a one-term, two-term trial. And I was with University College as a part-time enrolled, because it was less expensive. And seeing as it was coming out of my pocket, I had to do what I could do. Because I figured as long as I graduate, as long as I stay in school, I won't fall back too far. Because the realization hit me, there was no way I was going to graduate in four years . . . absolutely no way possible . . . so at least if I take one class, (1) I won't have to pay back my student loans right away—that's very important—and (2) I could try to help my GPA.

So, your income was on student's loans, that's what you put yourself through school with?

The problem was, I couldn't even get a student loan at that point. This is fall semester. I believe I just paid it in class for one class. Housing was a problem, but I don't remember how I did that. I didn't really answer any questions as far as housing was concerned. They were aware of my situation and everything and I paid as I could, I'll put it that way. But the main concern as to why I stayed in on campus housing at that point because I did not have the regular income so I could pay my rent and also the regular income so I could feed myself every week. So spring of 1991 rolls around. I end up registering for two courses instead of just the one and what I did, I was retaking some of the courses that I had failed because at that point I was still going to be back in engineering. That was my goal at that point. I was still going to be an aerospace engineer. Spring of 1991 comes around and I changed . . . I moved from south campus to north campus because I met this girl and she was aware of the facts—that Student Support Services, the NAACP Scholarship funding—and all that other kind of stuff, so she kind of got me back on the ball towards trying to stay in.

Now what year was she?

She was a freshman, actually. Part of the thing that I think that happened was that she had her mother come up with her her freshman year and her mother had the insight to look into all those different kinds of things. My mother, for one, did not come up with me. My father wasn't going to come because he is all the way in California.

You mean your freshman year or?

My freshman year.

You came by yourself?

Practically. What happened was we drove up—this is me, my uncle, my grandfather . . .they unloaded my boxes, patted me on the head, gave me a hug, and said 'bye. You know, that was the end of that. I basically had to learn everything completely on my own, you know, who to talk to, whatever. So this is now, once again, spring of 1991.

So you're beginning your third year here. And you were at what level, do you think?

At that point I was still a sophomore because of my GPA and I spoke with Mr. Boney—I forget exactly what he is—so you know, I had to pour out my heart to him, which was very difficult for me because there were a lot of personal things that were going on, and I didn't want to tell anybody at that point. But he got me through it. He made a few phone calls. He said "It sounds like you need somebody to give you a second chance." I remember he said that. I made a point of harping on I was going through a lot of personal difficulties. That's part of the reason my grades went the way they did. I also had medical proof that I was really ill because at that point my medical file at the Health Service had to be about an inch and a half thick. So, you know if it was that deep, I could always pull that one out. So, um, the thing that irritated me was back to the financial aid counselor. First of all she didn't get back in touch with me for the whole summer. She also neglected to tell me that I could come back to full-time status if I wanted to second semester. So, here I am, I am now stuck with this part-time status. Fortunately, because of Mr. Boney [Director, Division of Supportive Services], I ended up getting loans and things like that in part to help pay for my housing and for some of these classes and a couple of other things, but I was very mad and very offended with the fact that she neglected to tell me a few things here. So at that point, under Mr. Boney's suggestion, he said you need to go speak to some of these people. So I went to speak to the Director of Financial Aid to let him know there were some problems with these representatives. My financial aid counselor also got switched to another person who also helped me out. What else happened—I spoke with Ed Golden. He helped me out a little bit, not as much as Mr. Boney, but he helped me out a little bit. And that was pretty much it—I ended up getting my GPA for that semester back to about 2.5, 2.5 to 3.0, but that still didn't help my cum that much. The problem was, I was in a catch-22 at that point. I was at part-time status, not out of choice but because I had to, not just financially but academically. They were only going to let me take a certain amount of credits. The thing with University College, they wanted to keep me on part-time . . . not even 9 credits, I had to take a maximum of 6 credits because of my GPA. But my GPA was only going to grow so much if I can only take 6 credits. So, Mr. Boney made another phone call and he set me up with the Dean of Arts & Sciences, Barry Wells, so I went in and spoke with him and he gave me my second chance. So, what we had to do was flag a couple of grades to help my GPA up a little bit so that I had a 2.0 officially. That was for financial aid purposes and full-time status and all that other kind of stuff. With engineering, you know, I thought all that paperwork was ... you know, I wasn't going to come back to engineering until my GPA got to a certain thing and I had to take these classes and what have you. So it's now first semester . . . fall 1991 . . . so at that point I should have been a senior, but I was only a sophomore still. So I had that nice little sinking feeling, that lump in the pit of my stomach and everything, but I was just like, okay, fine. So, I took a lot of arts and sciences courses. I did very well. My GPA ended up being about a 2.5, which helped the 2.0 go up a little bit, and I was very indecisive at this point whether I still wanted to go back to engineering, and part of me says that engineering was doing their damnedest to keep me out of engineering because I had been to visit the Dean over there a couple of times to let him know what was in my mind as far as wanting to come back and what have you. First of all, it was difficult scheduling an appointment with him. Secondly, when I did get there, people were very snide to me, very crass, very contrite. I didn't appreciate it very much. I mean, it was just like they were throwing all their energies at me—"Go away, we don't want you, we don't want you, we don't want you"—in addition to the fact that when I went and I spoke with the advisor of the National Society of Black Engineers, they didn't even tell me anything. He told me that I needed to go back home. At that point, I couldn't even go back home because things were not that good between my mother and me. It was just better for me to stay here. So I thought he was very insensitive and unsupportive. I really saw that I had to do a lot of things by myself. So, that's cool, I'll do it by myself then— and I had suicidal thoughts a lot when I was going part-time because I had really hit an all-time low. But coming back to full-time helped me a lot, and it gave me a stronger sense of self that I really could do it especially at the end of that semester...

So at the end of that fall semester 1991, you were trying to decide whether to go back into engineering or stay in Arts & Sciences?

Right. And if I was going to stay in Arts & Sciences, what was I going to do? Because if you're 12 years old and you've known for your entire life and studied your entire life to be this aerospace engineer and all of a sudden you're 21 years old and you're like "Wow!—wait a minute—I haven't seen anything else, I haven't looked at anything else, but now I might have to. What am I going to do?" So, I spoke with a couple of career development people in Arts & Sciences, and I mean it was really weird the difference in staff and people being more open and communicative in Arts & Sciences versus Engineering which was incredible. It was almost like I had gone from Alaska to Hawaii. I think also part of it is really affected by the staff itself, because you go into engineering, the only woman you are going to see, except for one, if she is still here. I believe she is a chemical engineering professor . . . She's still here. You are going to see a whole bunch of old crony White men with the good ol' boy network. You are going to see secretaries that are female, but that's it. You're not going to see any Black faculty members. I mean, I had one TA who really helped me out, and he wasn't in aerospace—but he made a point of trying to help me out because he understood where I was coming from.

Was he African American?

Um, actually, I think he was African. I don't know, it was just the way he taught me was completely different. For some reason when I would go and I would study—because I really would study—it wouldn't work for me with other TAs because I was repeating this class this time. But the way he sat down and put things on paper and moved it around and helped out during recitations and everything and it just finally got through. I know some of it has to do with the fact it was a course I was repeating, but I looked at it in a completely different perspective, so I was trying to figure out whether that's subconscious psychologically or not that I now have somebody who is going to look upon me kindly—someone more willing, more ready to prepare myself to prepare these things—or if it was really that he was a good teacher. I mean, I already know he was a good teacher, but that color thing had a lot to do with it. I was thinking about going into Math Education at the end of fall of 1991, but I decided against it and decided to go with African American Studies. This is probably a couple of weeks into the spring 1992 semester. The reason why I did that was because I had always done well in my African American Studies courses. It was very important to me and, I don't know, I just got a high off of it. Of course, it was an easier way out at that point. You know, because I was thinking more in terms of graduation, financial aid and everything, because at the time, you know, financial aid has already made a point of telling me, like, "If you don't graduate by spring 1994, we can't do anything for you," even though it's not—I mean, part of this is my fault but not all of it—and I understand, you know, they have their standards and everything. Doesn't make it any easier on me... So, now I'm an African American

Studies major, minor in sociology, and I come home from classes smiling more right now. It's a lot of fun and it fascinates me. I remember earlier when I was a freshman, I was thinking to myself, you know these classes are nice and everything but it would bore me. It doesn't bore me as much as I thought it would. I think maybe it's because I am taking more of the 300–400 class levels versus the introductory. That might be part of it. I intend to get my master's in education, and I am going to get my doctorate in sociology.

So, have you gone completely away from engineering?

No more engineering for the next 5 to 7 years. It still fascinates me. I still like watching planes. I still like reading the books, and I still have some old textbooks because I just refuse to sell them back for sentimental reasons. I still like to look, but I can't do that right now. I'm going to leave it alone and come back to it later…

So, your field is going to be education?

Education. I want to be teaching at a university or a college, preferably, because I think you need a lot more faculty. . . A good example is Professor Paris. I've been in to speak with him a couple of times. I'm in his sociology class right now, that's Race, Class, and Power . . . and I let him know what is going on with me. But I was in there explaining to him what is going on with me, and he looked at me and he smiled and he nodded, and he got that nice little twinkle in his eye and said, "yes I've observed it's been a problem with particular people who look a certain way and have a certain background. The university does not look out in their best interests." So it was a lot better and also, I don't know, maybe it is because of the field, but my professors are so much more warm, so much more open. I feel that I can go talk to them anytime and I don't have to just talk to them about course work. I can just talk to them.

And are these your professors—Black, White and Asian, whatever?

Yeah, right now. I am also only taking African American Studies and sociology courses, so I'm going to go ahead and make that assumption that they have the understanding of where I come from to a certain extent, much better than somebody in engineering would, even though they probably do, but they aren't telling you.

The exasperation that these students felt as they talked about these acts of racism is clear. Dano was singled out and embarrassed, having his character called into question by a security guard because the color of his skin matched a generic description of a Black male suspect. Students considered this type of discrimination by security a highly visible form of racism. The security officer obviously bought into the stereotype of the Black male, i.e., criminal, threatening to White females, and treated Dano accordingly. This stereotype is perpetuated daily in the media. Black males have been stopped and questioned and/or arrested for no other reason than being in the wrong neighborhood after dark.

Dano explained that he was not the only Black male student who was mistaken to be a suspect. Talking with other Black males on campus, he learned that this scenario had happened to many of them, not because they fit the description in any other way than being Black and male. This type of treatment is common among Black males in a predominantly White environment.

The other, more subtle racism is the scenario Tirae related, that of being invisible, as if we didn't exist. She described a *women's studies* class where the professor did not see the value of discussing the work of Black women feminists. Assigning an article, and including it in the syllabus to be read, is not enough. In fact, once the article by Angela Davis had been assigned, not to require some discussion or analysis of it served to further trivialize or render the author invisible. Students' perspectives are formed by what they experience and in this instance the Black students perceived by the action of the professor and the inaction of the White students that little value is placed on the works of Black women. Tirae's comment about feeling more excluded in this women's studies class than in other situations on this campus alludes to the ongoing debate of Black women's invisibility in the women's movement. Further, this type of devaluation and invisibility of Blacks and their accomplishments in academe, fosters the sense of superiority in White students and condones their not learning about the contributions of other cultures.

Violet's experience is included as a student's perception of being both Black and a woman in a predominantly White male discipline at a predominantly White university. This is a classic example of what is termed "The fly in the buttermilk" syndrome. Here, Violet talks about the discomfort in knowing that her professor knew her by name, even though she had not met with him or the TA. Violet's question "Why do they know who I am?" indicates her fear of being an easy target for acts of discrimination. The feelings of intimidation and apprehension are akin to being under a microscope and having her every movement, good or bad, magnified. Understanding that there are many sides to each student's experience, I remind you that the students' perceptions were their reality at the time. Life choices were based on these perceptions. Violet left the university the semester after our interview, not having completed her degree program.

7

✣ A Different Perception of the Black Students' Experience

I asked four of the students who have reviewed their transcripts and given me feedback for clarity what I should do with their accounts of their experiences. They gave me permission to "tell them what it is really like," "tell it like it really is."

Let us be clear about institutional racism as we contemplate what these students have said about their experiences at a predominantly White university. Institutional racism, on the one hand, is similar to "beauty" in that it is "in the eye of the beholder." On the other hand, it can be likened to the "double-edged sword" whereby it benefits one and cuts down the other. Given the current data, the persons in the institution see their actions one way and the Black students see these actions (in the form of programs, policies, and interpersonal interactions) in a different way.

Institutional racism affects both the institution and students of color by altering the quality of interaction and the opportunities for social and academic success. From the point of view of the administration of institutions which provide recruitment and support programs for Black and underrepresented students, its actions are not racist. It has shown good faith and with the best of intentions. Racism, however, is not only overt acts of prejudice or projecting attributes onto another. Racism is a belief coupled with the feeling that certain groups or races are inherently superior to others, that one race is supreme (Schaefer, 1993). On a college campus, as in society, students are most challenged with the interactive effects of race and class.

According to Pinderhughes (1989), and I summarize, there are several basic tenets of racism:

1. Racism is a product of culture. People are *socialized* from an early age to think and behave in racist ways.
2. Racism is historical, having grown out of economic and political situations of the past.
3. Both Whites and people-of-color maintain racism. (p. 244)

Racism is learned behavior and is expeditiously passed on generation after generation within the policies and the laws government and institutions have made. Moreover, students, faculty, staff, and administrators of color, unbeknownst to themselves, take an active role in the institutionalization of racism in three distinct ways:

1. By identifying with the institution—assimilation and latent belief in the myths of group innate inferiority;
2. By focusing on culture and differences rather than challenging institutional policy;
3. By avoiding focus on race and attempting to achieve individual success. (p. 244)

The institution does not have to do anything to perpetuate the current level of racism within the institution. If it says, "We are going to do something," students must wait and see. In reality, incoming students will either go on with their educational program and graduate, or drop out and go somewhere else. The institution, for its part does not have to do anything differently. There will be a continuing turnover in students—students making protests, students expecting change—and the institution, by doing nothing, will maintain the status quo. A prime example, from the perspective of the students, was the African American Studies Department at Syracuse University not having a chairperson for such a long time, not hiring and not granting tenure to Black faculty in that department for years even though there was a "decision" to do so (*The Post Standard*, Feb. 4, 1989).

Institutional racism is not only detrimental to students of color, it also has an impact on Whites (Helms, 1992). The fact is that Whites are in the power majority now on campuses as well as in the larger society.

However, with the multiplication of multiethnic groups in America, the White establishment may not continue to enjoy this position indefinitely. White people are a part of the American melting pot whether they like it or not. Universities and other institutions maintain the perception that the White race is superior and thereby handicap other ethnic groups and races. Several scholars in *The Racial Crisis in American Higher Education* (Altbach & Lomotey, 1991) assert that universities are at the center of the social construction of reality. By maintaining the status quo the institution is producing inferior "work products" when it does not allow White students the opportunity for equality by advocating interactions with and education about other cultural groups and challenging them to become the best they can be.

For educational institutions, the mission should be to educate *all* students and have academic support for all, then the standards of the students who graduate must necessarily be raised. The result is that everybody will feel more productive and be able to interact in the global society. We must incorporate into our academic support for students both interpersonal awareness and accountability (Altbach & Lomotey, 1991). Students will be more confident and knowledgeable, and will leave the institution competent and prepared. This is not what is currently happening. Much of our current work force and newly unemployed are people who have dropped out, people who have tried college, and people who were not successful.

How Good Is Good Enough?

When entering college, the Black students featured in this study felt prepared to fit in to the academic arena. Even those who came from the most dense urban settings had done well in their high schools. They had prepared themselves by staying in school, doing their work, and graduating. Look at Arnie, J.R., Gail—all were honor students in high school. Their comments indicate that these students initially felt themselves prepared to pursue college level work in a predominantly White setting. The fact that the university recruited them confirmed, for the students, that they would be able to succeed. Or did it? Students spoke about their high school grades being "really good," having above an 85 average, a 4.0, and even being the valedictorian of the senior class. These students were honored to have been accepted, but they also felt they were good enough to succeed in such a setting. Several said that they expected to "have to work harder," but that comment was usually followed with a qualifier of sorts—"because *we* always have to work harder" or "because of the color of our skin." Chickering and Reisser (1993) note a cause for this accommodation: "When life presents challenges or new information that existing cognitive structures cannot handle, the resulting dissonance or disequilibrium forces a new accommodation or alteration of the cognitive structure" (p.7). Having also to make accommodations in the social environment was what stirred up emotions among these students.

Institutional policies and programs redefined these students as underprepared or educationally or socially disadvantaged (Yonai, 1991). Black students at the most prestigious predominantly White four-year public universities outperform their counterparts at less prestigious schools, even after controlling for socioeconomic background, achievement in high school, and other institutional characteristics (A. W. Smith, 1991, p. 111). I am not arguing the point of preparedness here. The point I am making is that of perceptions— the student perceptions of themselves and the perceptions others have of the students—and the actions that resulted from those perceptions.

On the one hand, students' academic preparedness often stood in direct contrast to their economic need for financial aid, to be able to attend a private university, or in some cases any institution of higher education. The guidelines for state and federal grant programs state that you must be "needy" to be funded, and in the history of these programs, particularly in the northeast, the recipients of grant programs, such as HEOP, have been disproportionately students of the African diaspora. The well-known phrase "Damned if you do, damned if you don't" comes to mind because Black students at this stage of development (and even many adults who may be the deciding parent in this case) see their options as a dichotomy—either "I can accept this grant and accept this opportunity" and be labeled, or "I will not be able to attend college because my family cannot raise the thousands of dollars to meet the costs of a college education."

On the other hand, as was the case in my study, half of the students were not initially admitted under programs for the economically disadvantaged and did not receive state or federal grants. Because they were Black students, good in math and science, they were (in some cases) supported by program staff and resources for underrepresented groups. Labels beget actions based on perceptions. These were superior students in their high schools who experienced the same treatment, malaise, and stigmas because of the perceptions others held about students of color.

A Different Perception of the Black Students' College Experience

As stated in chapter 3, the college experience for Black students is far more complex than existing theories of student development from adolescence to early adulthood have indicated. My depiction of "The Black Students' College Experience at a Predominantly White Institution" (Figure 7) is derived from students' data as related to their growth and development during their undergraduate years on campus.

Black Identity, as an integral part of Black student development from adolescence to adulthood, focuses on the Black experience during four or more years in college. Black students of college age have been through a pre-encounter stage prior to entering college—based on landmark studies (Brown vs. Board of Education), as early as preschool ages 3 and 4, and kindergarten (Cross, 1991). The experience of recognizing that you are being treated differently because of the color of your skin is one that happens when Black children in America begin to interact with persons outside of their immediate families.

GOAL CLARIFICATION
Personal Commitment
Re-remembering

VALIDATE IDENTITY
GOAL ASSESSMENT
Accepting "Who I am"
Commitment to self

IDENTITY CONFUSION
Searching for understanding of self
Affirming one's Blackness

INQUIRY / CAMPUS INCONGRUITY
The college campus as a melting pot
Sees the world as Black and White

Figure 7   THE BLACK STUDENTS' COLLEGE EXPERIENCE AT A PREDOMINANTLY WHITE INSTITUTION - *R. D. Davis © 1996*

Black students have gone through different kinds of anticipatory socialization (Merton, 1968; Weidman, 1989) and have been made aware of skin color differences in subtle ways as well as by policies and practices within our public school systems that were intended to help our urban children. Students in this study spoke about being groomed or made mentally ready to go to college because of the aspirations of parents or extended family members. They had been to the *right schools* in their communities and taken the *right courses* to prepare them to go on to college. Parents and school administrators were right in matters of education, and the student followed the expectations of these authorities. During their high school years, prior to coming to the university, Black students began to experience a *sense of competence*, the confidence in their ability to cope with what comes and to achieve successfully.

Inquiry/Campus Incongruity

As has been said, the first years of college are governed by dualistic perception (Perry, 1981) and is a time of both diffusion and isolation (Erikson, 1968). According to Erik Erikson,

> Identity formation thus goes beyond the process of *identifying oneself with others* in the one-way fashion... It is a process based on a heightened cognitive and emotional capacity to *let oneself be identified* [by concrete persons] as a circumscribed individual in relation to a predictable universe which transcends the circumstances of childhood. (emphasis in original, 1964, p. 90)

At this developmental stage, things are perceived as either right or wrong, good or bad, and basically derived from "authority." The first year is also a time when the Black student meets other Black and African American students from various backgrounds and inevitably begins to experience *what it's like to be a minority* (Rema) on a scale that could not have been imagined.

Being Black on a predominantly White campus involves two feelings in phase 1: first, excited curiosity and second, incongruity (Figure 7). In 1989, the incoming class of first-year students was a total of 3,189 students which included 2,369 White students and 203 African Americans (Syracuse University Center for the Support of Teaching and Learning). The number of White students, along with large introductory classes where there might be six or fewer Black students, was overwhelming to the students in this study. Living in close proximity to White students, in residence halls, was for all of them an educational experience, though not always a pleasant one. Observing the social life of White peers was informative for Black students as they began to also learn more about the African American heritage and make choices in their own lives.

According to Cross (1991), the Black individuals during an encounter stage are beginning to reinterpret the world as a consequence of the encounter and are in a testing position during which they carefully and with apprehension try to validate new perceptions. Coming to the college campus may have been the first time these students had confronted different interpretations of what it means to be "Black" because of differences in cultural norms based on where they were reared, parental ethnic origin, and citizenship. Many students had been recruited from the five Boroughs of New York, having a similar "Black cultural" experience in inner-city schools, similar music style preferences and more permissive city lifestyle. They met up with Black students from smaller, more suburban upstate New York cities or from rural towns, as well as Black students from other states and countries. All students had their own history in the way they talked, their family value structure, their perceptions of what it meant to be "Black." In their first year, students had to negotiate many relationships.

Students came back to school the second year with some understanding of the campus culture; of what was expected of them academically and socially. The institution was no longer making decisions for them in most instances. Parents were seen as supportive but distant, not understanding the confusion that their child was experiencing. It is probable that the students were not able to articulate their feelings at this point, particularly to their parents. Data indicate that all of the students experienced lower grades than they were used to achieving in one or both of their first-year semesters. They also talked about feeling unsure of themselves in that second year. Students were given the power (and according to the students, little academic advising) to make choices in their class work, in their social lives, in declaring a major.

Identity Confusion

Every student talked about taking an African American Studies (AAS) class either as classes in their major, as a minor, or as an elective "to really learn about our heritage" (Gail) or "just to be in a class where you didn't have to feel like you had to have your guard up" (Yoclee). However, more important was the bond the students said they felt with the other students in those AAS classes. Learning about themselves and their history gave students a connectedness that made the differences inconsequential. African Americans' contributions discussed in AAS classes provided role models for the struggle against racism, and for endurance and persistence. Students talked about finding themselves; "finding out who I am; finding my niche" I have called this period identity confusion—searching for understanding of self while attempting to affirm one's Blackness (Figure 7, phase 2).

For most students in this study, this was the time—some point between the second semester sophomore and end of first semester junior year (4th to 7th semester)—when they became aware of the changes they had been going through, as well as the mistakes they had made. They spoke of thinking about the effects of the things that had been happening in their lives, and the angry feelings they experienced and because of the racism that had been perpetrated against them. Many of the students, as the data indicate, exhibited retreat and escape behavior before deciding to persist to graduation. Remember Vern, who stopped out but returned to graduate, and Yoclee, who remained in school but decided in her junior year to change her major and proceed in another career.

Validate Identity/Goal Assessment

Perry (1981) refers to the transition of moving to relativism as "understanding that everything can not be equally right; that there are 'best' answers or better ways of looking at things" (p. 86). Similarly, the Black students experienced dissonance as they met the challenges, made the decisions. Having affirmed, for themselves, their Black Identity, their reason for being the person they had become (thus far) the students in their second interviews exuded confidence and were at the point of maturity where they were determined to graduate and do whatever was necessary (even when it meant another semester or year).

I contend that the Black student's development from adolescence to early adulthood embodies the additional burden of finding his/her identity as a Black person. It has been said that a transitory "negative identity" is often the necessary precondition for a truly positive and truly new one (Erikson, 1964, p. 97). Being at a predominantly White university magnifies this aspect of a student's development. Being Black among so many White and different students increases the *need*, not only the desire, to be with other Black people like yourself: students with similar values, coping skills, study habits, and aspirations. Given the individual Black student and her/his personal background (social and familial and academic) characteristics, the decision to commit to self reinforced each person's decision to persist to graduation or to take another path.

Goal Clarification

Nine of the students participated in a second interview in their senior year or later—two were interviewed after graduation. At this point students talked about having made up their minds to get on with the business of graduating. They said they owed it to themselves, their families, and the people back home. Personal commitment was the theme that ran through these second interviews. A commitment to follow through in the face of the racism. They spoke with a confidence that they would be able to go and work in any arena because they had been able to make it in this predominantly White university.

Interestingly, students connected their success at this university to the struggles of the African American forefathers and foremothers. Black students on campus during the early 1990s used a metaphor of "putting on the armor" for preparation to go to classes and interactions with staff in the various offices. However, they said it helped to remember the struggles that had taken place to make it possible for interracial education to happen because, by remembering they would remember to recommit themselves to continue to be role models for younger siblings and friends. This re-remembering as a concept has been discussed in literary circles by Poet Laureate Toni

Morrison as an ability to visualize events (the struggles of slavery, family struggles, even people) that, even though you were not there, the meaning of the event is as clear as if you were. Students, individually, remembered what it meant to their families (extended kinship) to get an education in memory of a time when it was forbidden.

I present Figure 7 as a work in progress born of the experiences of eighteen students and look forward to opportunities to continue qualitative investigation of the Black and "other" student experience of persistence on predominantly White campuses and a comparative look at student experiences at historically Black colleges and universities.

8

✣ Interpretations

Why are Black students achieving at a lower rate and graduating at a much lower percentage rate than White students at predominantly White institutions? Why is this the case even at institutions that have supportive services and staffs specifically designated for the student who is educationally and economically disadvantaged? What is it that makes these two questions seem like one? Could it be the widely held stereotype that the majority of students with "educational and economic disadvantages" are Black and poor? Even though this scenario is not true, in America Black students continue to be treated as if they all need to be remediated to meet standards historically set by White educators. The gap is widening between who enters and who graduates from our institutions of higher education, and dropout rates are increasing.

I wanted to hear the students' side of the story and, therefore, began this study with four research questions from the concerns stated above:

1. How do Black students perceive their college experience at a predominantly White institution?
2. What is the importance of the Summer Institute (a precollege six-week summer academic residence program) to the decision to persist to graduation?
3. What are some of the other reasons, as perceived by these students, why Black students persist to graduation?

4. Are there common themes among the students' experiences? If so, could these themes provide insights for developing interventions to increase the graduation rates of Black students?

Data presented here furnish several answers in the form of how the students felt about the educational environment. This discussion also generated new questions, and caused us to revisit existing questions and the answers usually given to them.

How Do Black Students Perceive Their College Experience at a Predominantly White Institution?

There are phrases that indicate the wide range of experiences these Black students had: "hurtful," "an eye-opener," "preparation for the real world," "racist," "a very good social environment," and so forth. If we take only the phrases, we miss the quality of the experiences. This quality was aptly expressed in the longer quotes included in earlier chapters of this study. As I reviewed these experiences, I realized one of the main things that the students talked about, particularly in their initial interviews, was the difficulty they experienced in the day-to-day negotiations on campus, i.e., in their residence life, in their classrooms, and in their interactions with the financial aid processes.

When I interviewed students the second time, I had already looked at the transcripts from the first interviews and noticed very specifically that the students did not talk as much about the White students as they did about themselves and their interactions. There was not a lot of hostile "I hate Whites" language, such as had been heard on campus from Black student advocates during the years 1988 to 1991—the early years the students featured in this study were at the university. Particularly, in the second interviews, students talked about the differences between Black students and White students and about being treated differently from their White peers on this predominantly White campus. They reported some of the hurtful things that happened, that could only happen to a Black person.

Johanna, in chapter 4, told about her three roommates who seemed to do the college life effortlessly, while she had to struggle in her aloneness. Gail also talked about a roommate who wanted to touch her hair, and who was amazed that Gail could brush her hair the same way that White students do. Gail's comments also point out how segregated from other cultures some White students have been:

> So I was just in the lottery or whatever. She was from Connecticut. She was a really nice person. I don't want to say that she didn't have any Black friends but it was like a culture shock to her. She was just like, "Oh, wow, look at your hair, can I touch it?" I was like, "Would you give me a break! Go away." . . . She was just like, "Oh, cool, oh my gosh, you even do this like I do." It seemed like she wanted to say that more or less, I mean, like, "Wow, you think just like me." But, in the beginning I hung out with her and everything because I didn't really know anyone else... And I was just miserable with this girl. She was awful. She was really nice though.

Gail was annoyed that White students would not have any more information about a different culture, particularly the African American culture, because that cultural group is not new to the United States. However, Gail had mixed emotions because this young woman was her roommate with whom she obviously had some things in common such as gender, chronological age, and possibly some likes and dislikes.

The male students, specifically Arnie and J. R., talked about competition. They both began in the School of Engineering. They both came to the institution to get their education so they could get a good job to be able to go out into the big corporate world and make money, not unlike a lot of other students. Both Black males—one on an HEOP scholarship, the other being supported by his parents—were admitted into their professional school (Engineering) on the basis of their prior academic achievements. They expected college to be more difficult than high school but not for the reasons they encountered. Though their reasons differed, both found a lack of support and understanding of their problems within the school, as well as among peers in the Black student chapter of the National Society of Black Engineers.

Students talked about the importance of being a "Greek" versus a "non-Greek." Within the Greek fraternal and sororal realm, there are four traditional Black sororities and four traditional Black fraternities, as well as the predominantly White sororities and fraternities. Black students in the population I interviewed, who decided to join a sorority or fraternity, chose Black sororities and fraternities. There are students who are of the African diaspora who prefer to join White fraternities and White sororities. Jay Jay is the one who put it into words, and he said "It is just what you are comfortable with." Students who selected White sororities and fraternities were students who were "comfortable with mingling with and interacting with White students." Students who joined the Black fraternities did not [necessarily] feel uncomfortable with Whites, rather they preferred to be with Blacks, particularly for fraternity brother and sorority sister relationships.

Then there was the student discussion about the schism between the Greeks and the non-Greeks. Some students who were Greek felt "that they were 'all that,'" which was the way Tirae explained the ubiquitous Greek elitism that she mentioned but did not dwell upon. Vern had very definite preconceived notions about what it meant to be in a sorority where sister-talk is kept among sisters. Being an only child, however, having neither lived nor interacted with other women in a sister-like manner, she fell into traps that betrayed the confidentiality of the sisterhood with consequences that were devastating for her. As a result, she decided to drop out in December 1988. However, she returned to full-time study (a year and a half later) in the fall of 1991. During our first interview (January 1992) Vern talked about going back home, going to another college and trying to put her life together, still constantly seeking the education that would make her able to go out into the world as an independent person. She ended up coming back to Syracuse University because of the credibility that the degree would have. Vern also returned because of the community relationships she had formed. The Black community that she had belonged to in the City of Syracuse was always welcoming to her. She felt supported. She was able to come back, even though she still had to decide what it was she wanted to do. Vern was able to return to a supportive environment, living off campus in the community that had befriended her.

This sense of belonging was central in the students' discussion of finding their place at the university. They looked for "their Black community" on and off campus. Tirae and Dano spoke about how difficult it was to find their "niche" on campus in their early years. Tirae saw the activism of the S.A.S. and believed very strongly that they should take the administration to task over the AAS Department. However, with regard to her own involvement at that time she said:

> I really wasn't involved in a lot of student organizations. I would go to some of the S.A.S. meetings and at that time Quentin was president who was a very strong leader on campus. I listened to what he had to say, but I don't know exactly if I was ready to deal with it, to grasp it. Because you know if you are not raised in that type of environment, then it is still new to you.

Dano, in his senior reflection talked about how important joining [belonging] had been to him as a Black student:

> The second semester I was definitely joining student organizations and defending the constituency... I was experiencing a sense of just BLACK, being Black. And that mentality created a whole Black consciousness. But it's here on the campus at Syracuse, because it is such a White, predominantly White European university that we are forced to come together. And all the [Black] student groups are forced to kind of stick together.

Yoclee and Vern made the point that families in the Black community outside of the campus were safe havens to Black students and Dano said, "You know, I feel more comfortable. I feel like a small boy just chillin out." Students needed to be comfortable in their understanding of the norms of social interactions both on the White campus and off campus in the Black community.

There has been an interdisciplinary discussion among scholars on the biculturalism of Black and African American young people. (Ogbu, 1981; Spencer et al., 1985; Pinderhughes, 1989; Irvine, 1991; Steele, 1992; Hollins, 1994; King, 1994). John Ogbu, in 1981, proposed a "cultural-ecological model of inner-city childrearing and development," which resonates with my understanding of the bicultural nature of the experiences of the students in my study. For clarity Elaine Pinderhughes's (1989) definition suffices: "Biculturalism [is] the ability to live in two worlds to tolerate the associated conflicts in cultural values and cultural practices" (p. 181).

Children of color learn about the social norms of Whites at an early age because the social norms in America are based on White Anglo Saxon Protestant definitions of values etiquette, civility, and manners. Conflicts in residence life, accusations of separatism, and daily aggravations—as reflected in the *Daily Orange* Opinion columns and hall meetings—were indications that White students had not learned from previous interaction about the social cultural norms of Black students. Growing up in these two separate and, for all practical purposes, segregated cultures, most Whites don't ever have to interact with Blacks unless it is by choice in the business world, but Blacks don't have that option. They have to interact with Whites, but they are not socializing with Whites. However, it is as important for Whites to learn about the many realities of Black culture as it is for Blacks to know the social norms of Whites. As the situation is today, many White students lead their lives prior to college without substantive interactions with people from other cultures. A university campus offers the opportunity for such interactions, thus providing students with a better understanding of the diversity of our global, multicultural society. Without this understanding, students are not truly educated to enter the work force of the twenty-first century.

Differences (e.g., in perception and in treatment) in the classroom were also an issue for these students. They talked about the differences that the other students made in the classroom, as well as differences made by the faculty. Gail, in particular, talked about the faculty as being very supportive. Her perspective was that students should initiate interactions, that faculty and TAs would answer their questions. In that regard she expected that faculty should know her. She managed very well and was able to complete her program of study in four years feeling that she had been supported in her academic life. Gail was the student who had attended only private schools because her parents did not want her to be undereducated in public schools. In the private school environment Gail learned firsthand the nuances of faculty-student interaction.

Conversely, Tirae, Celeste, Violet, Kasey, Johanna, and Rema gave specific instances where differences in treatment occurred, where they experienced discomfort or felt put-upon or slighted because of the color of their skin. This does not mean that none of these students had school experiences similar to Gail's. Tirae, Johanna, and Violet mentioned accelerated, advanced placement classes although not specifically private school experience. However, based on their less than positive interactions with faculty I conclude that their understanding of the "proper" way to engage faculty support was different from Gail's.

Freddie, Gail, and Johanna, who connected in the choir, spoke of the Black Celestial Choral Ensemble (BCCE) as a "family" away from home. Of the students I interviewed, one male and three females were in BCCE beginning in freshman year. They saw the choir as providing the structure, academic support, camaraderie, and cultural connection necessary for them to succeed. This unit was very demanding, with a regular rehearsal schedule and performances. Regarding students' academic schedules, students found that, even though they were not all in the same majors, they were supportive of the need to study and sensitive to the concerns about classroom interactions. They had study circles in conjunction with rehearsal. Students bonded socially, culturally, and academically.

Yoclee, however, did not find the same kind of unit or group that was supportive to her. In her interview she talked about the differences among the Black students, those students who did not come from the same place that she came from, and how they had discussions about who was better, who was more right in the ways that they behaved in public.

Black women students felt that the young White women they knew "came to the university just to get husbands." They weren't interested in any particular program. It was Randi who voiced an annoyance with the fact that these young White women were there and they "weren't serious about . . . working with people in communities or anything. They just wanted to be there, look pretty and meet their husbands." Now, for Randi, this was annoying because her purpose for coming to the university was to get an education so that she would be "able to be an independent person," and give back to her community, "particularly the children." There have been studies that have referenced specific gender and racial differences among female students (Holland & Eisenhart, 1990; Fleming, 1984). For example, Holland and Eisenhart in *Educated in Romance* discuss the nuances of both the inter- and intra-personal relationships of White and Black college women. Clearly this was not the intent of my study.

Though I did not do interviews with White students to find out why they came to campus, I did ask the students in this study why they chose this institution. In most cases, the answer was because of the credibility of the degree once they went out into the job market. However, they did not see any choices. They did not seem to feel that they had the choice to just stop going to school, to quit because it was too hard, to quit because of the racism, or to quit because of the way the Financial Aid Office treated them. Student after student talked about being on financial hold as being a fact of life at this campus. Whether students receive government financial aid or Syracuse University merit-based funds, there was a lot of red tape that went along with the financial aid. According to Kasey, Celeste, and Violet there was nothing to say that if you did every single bit of the paper work and filed it on time that it was going to be processed in an efficient manner, without hassle. Hassles over financial aid were a fact of life for many college students—Black and White. The fact that racism exists compounded the Black students' frustration with the bureaucracy.

What Is the Importance of the Summer Institute to the Decision to Persist to Graduation?

I began my study with students selected from the 1989 Summer Institute class, and I quickly discovered the importance of that experience for the students. The relevance of and the stability provided by the Summer Institute was reiterated in every interview. "Friendships," "support," "a place to come back to" is how the students described the base that the Summer Institute represented. It is important to note that the initial interviews were done when these students were second-semester sophomores or first-semester juniors. They were already successful as persisters according to the definition used by Yonai (1991) as she looked at the effectiveness of the Summer Institute on student persistence into the sophomore year—"For this study [Yonai's] persistence is defined as re-enrollment at Syracuse University for the fall semester following the freshman year" (p. 11). Nine of the eighteen students in the current study participated in the Summer Institute. I asked students what importance the program had for each of those who were in it. There was consensus on three points:

- Academic readiness—they came back to the campus in the fall knowing how to use campus resources, where to find services and get questions answered.
- Camaraderie—which students defined as "a Posse"—friends they could depend on. Each student spoke of the foundation they received, the lasting friendships that were formed.
- Esteem, dignity, values—the words were elaborate and yet simple in their meaning. Trust, "belief in me," expectations. Although students in this group remembered their REM professor [a Black professor] specifically from that summer they referred to the staff in a larger context over the four years. This staff—in the Division of Supportive Services—was there for the students when they needed services, jobs, and Tender Loving Care when "the going got rough.

Even students who did not attend the Summer Institute mentioned these qualities they had witnessed either vicariously or personally during their college career. In 1989, the services provided by the Division of Supportive Services programs were available free of charge or on a sliding fee schedule to any "minority" student meeting the educational or economic criteria. As mentioned earlier, however, there was a stigma attached to being "on those programs" much like the stigma of being "on welfare." Therefore, there were students who did not avail themselves of supportive services, even though they heard how helpful they were. Since 1992, many changes have been made to make tutorial and counseling services available to all students who have a need.

What Are Some of the Reasons, as Perceived by These Students, Why Black Students Persist to Graduation?

Persistence, for the purpose of this study, was defined as continuous enrollment at Syracuse University from the 1989 fall semester through graduation or through December 1993. Students were not asked about persistence per se. The open-ended questions were responded to with the expectations, disappointments, hopes, dreams, and realities of the students' experiences. The disparity in treatment by the university staff, faculty, and students was unexpected. The students were most angered by what they felt were racist acts because these were Black students of the 1980s whose parents and previous generations marched and fought for quality in education for Black students. These students thought, in 1989, that if they qualified for and were accepted into a predominantly White university, they could expect to and would receive the same kind of attention and education as any White student, as long as they did their part. They came prepared to do their part. However, they felt they were treated differently initially because they did not know the rules. Even with the advantages they felt they had gained from the Summer Institute experience, students by the second semester began to question their ability, measured by course grades, to fit in on this campus. By that second semester three of the students had GPAs below 2.0, which is at probation status. The other fifteen, whose cumulative grades were above 2.5, were not achieving at the level they had in high school. Freshman surveys have shown this to be a normative situation due to the transition to college life, but these students were not reassured on this point. They felt the pressure of both their families' and their communities' expectations, as well as the stereotypical notions of Whites that they could not achieve.

Eleven of the eighteen students whom I interviewed were first-generation college students. They did not have family members who had been to college before, so there was no one to tell them what to look out for, what things to expect and not to take personally. When we look at Violet, who was a second-generation college student on one side of the family and third generation on the other, was her college life any more pleasant? In fact, no, it was not. Violet, unlike her female family role models, chose to enter a male-dominated field of study whereas her mother and grandmother had both been teachers—traditionally a female-dominated field at the elementary level. Her father, however, who was successful in county government, having the distinction of being the first or one of a few, withdrew his moral and financial support when Violet said her need to be supported was greatest.

Arguably, Violet had a more difficult time in the School of Engineering than the male students did. There is an indication from her interview transcript that she was treated differently because she was both female and Black. The males' interviews, however, support the fact that engineering was a very difficult place to be if you were a Black student. Students believed faculty intended to weed out the people they thought did not measure up to their standards, and the students felt they were not given an equal chance in relation to White students.

Violet also had health problems, among them mononucleosis. [I have known graduate students who had "mono" and it cost them a year of their graduate program. It is a disease that takes away the energy you need in order to be able to study and to do well in your academic pursuit.] However, because she chose not to tell her family about the effect her illness was having on her academics, she did not get support from those family members who could have been supportive. Violet also did not join any organizations on campus. She may have gone to a meeting or two, but she was not a part of a supportive Black organization. She felt, as she put it, "alone, fighting the battles alone." It was not until a freshman student, who came with the support of her parents, told her how to negotiate the system, that she began to truly fight back and fight for the education she felt she deserved.

Casey and Tirae talked about the insensitivities of the White students in their classrooms. They were both in political science, and they both felt the White students—who were going to be among the leaders in the next generation, "the power brokers, the politicians, negotiating in the government"—these students were "ignorant" (this was the term that the students used) of cultures other than their own and had no intention of learning what they could about other cultures. In chapter 5, I included Tirae's transcript where she talked about the two instances where she, as a Black student, took the responsibility to say "no," there are other people in the world besides just European Americans.

Dano talked about a different type of mistreatment. The institutionalized racism within the Security Department, in 1989 at Syracuse University, was such that students were being accosted, questioned, and taken to the security office based on a very nebulous, vague description of a tall Black man who was suspected of having committed a crime. That is not to say that all Black male students were tall and dark, but there were many of them who talked of having been stopped by Security, asked questions, asked their whereabouts, interrogated as it were. Even if they fit the description, so did thousands of other people. In chapter 7, I have included Dano's recounting of the situation that happened to him less than two months after he came to the Syracuse campus.

Dano went on to say that because of that incident in 1989 and the fact that it happened in the administrative office of Minority Affairs, there were some changes made in the security department and that, over the years (between 1989 and 1992 when Dano was interviewed), security had cleaned up their act and been renamed Campus Safety Department. He did not know how deep the changes were, but he gave security credit for at least attempting not to continue to be guilty of harassment.

The Black students talked about academic advisors and, as a group, they talked about the absence of advising. Of the eighteen students, sixteen reported they had poor, disinterested academic advisement until they got into their majors. Circumstances were different for individual students, but the students did not report having good advisement. Based on actions of the institution in 1992 and 1993, including the forming of a task force to look at how academic advisors could be better trained to work with students who were in difficulty, we do take note that the administration and the faculty were aware that there were problems in the academic advising students received and began the process of making meaningful changes. The students who started in 1989 did not benefit from those changes, however.

The students' expectation to graduate was heard in their choice of majors and their plans for graduate school. Three students had plans for and subsequently went to law schools. Career choices in economics, political science, and nursing indicated that these students had a vision of the future. This was illustrated, for instance, by Arnie's frustration and determination to stay in college until he got focused and then to graduate with his self-esteem intact. Data suggest also a deeper belief in "there being a reason for me being here." Students shared the dreams of their families. They were "supposed" to finish college. Whether they were second- or third-generation college students or the first, as was the case for eleven of the eighteen student participants, there were people back home who were expecting these Black students to graduate. The stress, emotional, psychological, and social, for students who "make it" to college, distinguishing themselves as the first in their family to go to college, can be harmful. In many ways, however, the students believed the daily challenges to be instructive and preparatory for life.

Are There Common Themes Among the Students' Experiences? If So, Could These Themes Provide Insights for Developing Interventions to Increase the Graduation Rates of Black Students?

I have already mentioned financial aid, but it is not only the financial aid staff whom the students talked about as acting differently toward them than they did toward other students. The students talked about being suspect. They talked about having the feeling that they were *not* expected to achieve. That feeling was reinforced when students were put into remedial classes without a firm reason. The reason they were put into these classes seemed to be because they were Black or Hispanic or Native American or Asian American. White students who entered the university under HEOP program guidelines of economically disadvantaged were also required to take these remedial classes. The criteria used in 1989, based on government guidelines and Syracuse University policies, is reviewed in chapter 2 under "The Students." The prevailing perception in the institution seemed to be that HEOP students were going to have a hard time in the academy. The students felt as though the institution was always trying to make them adjust. They came expecting to mature and to grow, but not to have to adjust to fit into a narrowly defined role that someone else had set up for them.

Earlier in the study I talked about the students from the city versus students who came from other places. I mention it again here [and in the present tense since it is also a current situation] because of the many studies that have been done that say that students' background characteristics—what they bring to the University—has a bearing on how they are able to succeed. Where students "come from" was and is important here, in the context of retention and persistence, because Syracuse University recruits very heavily from the New York and New Jersey area. Students in these major urban areas have had a much greater exposure than students from rural and suburban areas to multicultural living, languages from other countries, and opportunities to understand the norms and mores of cultures other than their own. They have become familiar, of course, with the White power structure. The Black student who comes from Chicago, Cincinnati, Los Angeles, or any of the major metropoles should also be able to negotiate the diverse student population on the Syracuse University campus.

However, those students in my study who came from small towns in New York State, rural towns in the Midwest and Southwest, and foreign countries—for instance Maria, from a small rural town—had a perception and stereotype of the New York City Black students. These stereotypes were not ones born out of experience, but out of the video personification and objectification on television. In situation comedies, music videos, and even in dramatic shows the Black man or woman is often portrayed as either the buffoon or the victim (Black on Black crime) or perpetrator of violence. These less experienced students, Black and White, because of their ignorance-based fear of interaction, did not associate with Black students from the cities, did not engage in conversation and, in many cases, went out of their way not to be in groups with Black students. This last statement was not the case with Maria who suffered because she actively tried to be included and nurture her African American heritage.

The Black students continually said that they got tired of educating. They wondered why it was that the Black students had the responsibility to educate Whites about their lifestyle when "we had to know about the lifestyle of Whites." Black people had to learn that in their childhood, and they had to learn it to survive in today's world.

Black students expected that they were going to have to work hard but were dismayed when they arrived to discover that they did not have the study skills necessary to do well in college. This was the beginning of a pattern of self-doubt that most students experienced during their first and second semester. In every case, students did not perform as well their freshman year as they were accustomed to performing academically. As indicated by the several different Freshman Support Programs initiated since 1989 (*Black Issues in Higher Education* (1991), this period of adjustment is difficult for all students. Tinto (1975) called this the separation stage. Concerns over whether or not they fit in socially, in the academic arena, and within their own reference group surfaced. Students and their families thought these Black students were adequately prepared for life on a predominantly White campus. Merton (1968) called this process *anticipatory socialization*, a process of acquiring values and orientations found in statutes and groups in which one is not yet engaged but hopes one day to enter. However, students were ill-prepared for the depth of the institutionalized racism that confronted them in every aspect of their college experience.

This chapter explored the implications of the processes Black students must work through to persist to graduation in a predominantly White institution of higher education. Therefore, my purpose in this chapter was to raise the level of consciousness of college students, faculty, administrators, and staff about how institutionalized racism continues to exist and how it affects the lives and development of Black, White, and Biracial students on predominantly White college and university campuses.

✤ References

Adler, P. A., & Adler, P. (1991). *Backboards and blackboards*. New York: Columbia University Press.

Ajzen, I., & Fishbein, M. (1977). Attitude-behavior relations: A theoretical analysis and review of empirical research. *Psychological Bulletin, 84,* 888–918.

Ajzen, I., & Fishbein, M. (1972). Attitude and normative beliefs as factors influencing behavioral intentions. *Journal of Personality and Social Psychology, 21*(1), 1–9.

Allen, W. R. (1984). Race consciousness and collective commitment among Black students on White campuses. *Western Journal of Black Studies, 8*(3), 156–166.

Allen, W. R., Epps, E. G., & Haniff, N. Z. (Eds.). (1991). *Colleges in Black and White: African American students in predominantly white and in historically Black public universities*. Albany: State University of New York Press.

Altbach, P. G., & Lomotey, K. (Eds.). (1991). *The racial crisis in American higher education*. Albany: State University of New York Press.

American Council on Education, Office of Minorities in Higher Education. (1992). *Eleventh Annual Report on Minorities in Higher Education*. Washington, DC: D. J. Carter and R. Wilson.

Anzaldúa, G. (1990). *Making face, making soul Haciendo caras: Creative and critical perspectives by feminists of color*. 1st ed. San Francisco: Aunt Lute Foundation Books.

Armstrong-West, S., & de la Teja, M. (1988). Social and psychological factors affecting the retention of minority students. In M. Terrell & D. Wright (Eds.). *From survival to success: Promoting minority student retention*. Washington, DC: National Association of Student Personnel Administrators (pp. 25–53).

Asante, M. K., & Noor Al-Deen, H. S. (1984). Social interaction of Black and White college students: A research report. *Journal of Black Studies*, 14 (4), 507–516.

Astin, A. W. (1975). *Preventing students from dropping out.* San Francisco: Jossey-Bass.

Astin, A. W. (1977). *Four critical years: Effects of college on beliefs, attitudes, and knowledge.* San Francisco: Jossey-Bass.

Astin, A. W. (1982). *Minorities in higher education: Recent trends, current prospects, and recommendations.* San Francisco: Jossey-Bass.

Astin, A. W. (1990). *The Black undergraduate: Current status and trends in the characteristics of freshmen.* Los Angeles: University of California, Graduate School of Education.

Bean, J. P. (1983). The application of a model of turnover in work organizations to the student attrition process. *Review of Higher Education*, 6(2), 129–148.

Bean, J. P. (1990). Understanding why students stay or leave. In D. Hossler et al. (Eds.) *The strategic management of college enrollments.* San Francisco: Jossey-Bass.

Bean, J. P., & Metzner, B. (1985). A conceptual model of nontraditional undergraduate student attrition. *Review of Education al Research*, 55(4), 485–540.

Bentler, P. M., & Speckart, G. (1979). Models of attitude-behavior relations. *Psychological Review*, 86(5), 452–464.

Bentler, P. M., & Speckart, G. (1981). Attitudes 'cause' behaviors: A structural equation analysis. *Journal of Personality and Social Psychology*, 40(2), 226–238.

Blackwell, J. E. (1981). *Mainstreaming outsiders: The production of Black professionals.* Bayside: General Hall.

Bogdan, R. C., & Biklen, S. K. (1982). *Qualitative Research for Education.* Boston: Allyn and Bacon, Inc.

Brown vs Board of Education, 347 U.S. 483 (1954). United States Supreme Court.

Buttny, R. (1995). Talking race on campus: Reported speech sequences of racism and interracial contact on a university campus. Paper presented at the Georgetown University Conference, Advances in Discourse Analysis, Washington, DC.

Cabrera, A. F., Castaneda, M. B., Nora, A., & Hengstler, D. (1992) The convergence between two theories of college persistence. *Journal of Higher Education*, 63(2), 143–164.

Carter, D., & Wilson, R. (1992). *Minorities in Higher Education.* Washington DC: American Council on Education, annually published, 1992.

Chestang, L. W. (1972). Character development in a hostile environment. (Occasional Paper No. 3). Chicago: University of Chicago Press.

Chickering, A. (1969). *Education and Identity.* San Francisco: Jossey-Bass.

Chickering, A. W., & Reisser, L. (1993). *Education and Identity* (2nd ed.). San Francisco: Jossey-Bass.

Chronicle of Higher Education (1992). Almanac. August 26, 1992.

Cope, R., & Hannah, W. (1975). *Revolving college doors: The causes and consequences of dropping out, stepping out, and transferring.* New York: Wiley.

Cross, W. E. Jr. (1978). Models of psychological nigresence: A review. *Journal of Black Psychology*, 5, 13–31.

Cross, W. E. Jr. (1991). *Shades of Black: Diversity in African-American identity.* Philadelphia: Temple University Press.

Daily Orange, Syracuse University. September 11, 1989, pp. A-1, A-4.

Davis, R. B. (1991). Social support networks and undergraduate student academic-success-related outcomes: A comparison of Black students on Black and White campuses. In W. R. Allen, et al. (Eds.). *Colleges in Black and White: African American students in predominantly White and in historically Black public universities.* Albany: State University of New York Press (pp. 143–160).

Davis, R. D. (1996). African American students' perspectives of their experiences at a predominantly White institution: A qualitative piece of the retention puzzle. Syracuse University, 1996. UMI Dissertation Abstracts, Inc.

Deskins, D. R., Jr. (1991). Winners and losers: A regional assessment of minority enrollment and earned degrees in U.S. colleges and universities, 1974–1984. In W. R. Allen et al. (Eds.). *Colleges in Black and White: African American students in predominantly Black public universities.* Albany: State University of New York Press. (pp. 17–39).

Erikson, E. H. (1964). *Insight & responsibility: Lectures on the ethical implications of psychoanalytic insight.* New York: W. W. Norton.

Erikson, E. H. (1968). *Identity, youth and crisis.* New York: W. W. Norton.

Feldman, K., & Newcomb, T. (1969). *The impact of college on students.* San Francisco: Jossey-Bass.

Fleming, J. (1981). Special needs of Blacks and other minorities in the modern American college. In A. Chickering et al. (Eds.) *The modern American college: Responding to the new realities of diverse students and a changing society.* San Francisco: Jossey-Bass.

Fleming, J. (1984). *Blacks in College: A comparative study of students' success in Black and in White institutions.* San Francisco: Jossey-Bass.

Fordham, S., & Ogbu, J. U. (1986). Black students' school success: Coping with the "burden of acting white." *The Urban Review,* 18(3), 179–205.

Gibbs, J. T. (1973). Black students/White university: Different expectations. *Personnel and Guidance Journal,* 51(7), 463–469.

Gibson, M. A., & Ogbu, J. U. (1991). *Minority status and schooling: A comparative study of immigrant and involuntary minorities.* New York: Garland Publishing, Inc.

Giddings, P. (1988). *In search of sisterhood: Delta Sigma Theta and the challenge of the Black sorority movement.* 1st ed. New York: Morrow.

Glaser, B., & Strauss, A. L. (1967). *The discovery of grounded theory: Strategies for qualitative research.* Chicago: Aldine.

Gruin, P., & Epps, E. (1975). *Black consciousness, identity, and achievement: A study of students in historically Black colleges.* New York: John Wiley & Sons.

Hare, B. (1991). Beyond 'Black' students and 'White' universities. *The NEA Higher Education Journal.* 7(2), 157–159.

Helms, J. (1984). Towards a theoretical explanation of the effects of race on counseling: A Black and White model. *The Counseling Psychologist*, 12(4), 153–164.

Helms, J. (Ed.). (1990). *Black and White racial identity: Theory, research, and practice.* New York: Greenwood Press.

Helms, J. (1992). *A race is a nice thing to have: A guide to being a White person or understanding the white persons in your life.* Topeka, KS: Content Communications.

Helms, J. E., & Parham, T. A. (1990). The relationship between Black racial identity attitudes and cognitive styles. In J. E. Helms (Ed.), *Black and White racial identity: Theory, research, and practice.* New York: Greenwood Press.

Hill, R. (1986, July 27). Black leadership: A tradition at SU. *Syracuse Herald American*, pp. E-1, E-4.

Holland, D. C., & Eisenhart, M. A. (1990). *Educated in romance: Women's achievement, and college culture.* Chicago: The University of Chicago Press.

Hollins, E. R. (1994a, April). The burden of acting white revisited: Planning school success rather than explaining school failure. Paper presented at AERA annual meeting, New Orleans.

Hollins, E. R. (1994b). Teaching culturally diverse students: Applying the wisdom of practice. New York: Longman Publishing Group.

Irvine, J. J. (1991). *Black students and school failure: Policies, practices, and prescriptions.* New York: Praeger.

King, J. E. (1994, April). Perceiving reality in a new way: Rethinking the Black/White duality of our time. Paper presented at AERA annual meeting, New Orleans.

King, J. E. (1995). Culture-centered knowledge: Black studies curriculum transformation and social action. In J. A. Banks and C. A. McGee Banks (Eds.). *Handbook for research on multicultural education.* New York: MacMillan.

Lang, M., & Ford, C. A. (Eds.) (1988). *Black student retention in higher education.* Springfield: Charles C. Thomas.

Lewis, D. L. (Ed.). (1995). *W. E. B. DuBois: A reader.* New York: Henry Holt and Company, Inc.

Merton, R. K. (1968). *Social theory and social structure.* Revised ed. New York: Free Press.

Morrison L. (1989). The Lubin House experience: A model for the recruitment retention of urban minority students. In J. C. Elam (Ed.), Blacks in Higher Education: Overcoming the odds (pp. 11–27). Lanham, MD: University Press of America, Inc.

Morrison, L. (1992). An examination of the relationship of preadmission and institutional factors to college cumulative grade point average for "average achieving" high school students who became "above average achieving" college students. (Doctoral Dissertation. Syracuse University, 1992). *Dissertation Abstracts International*, 54(8).

Mow, S. L., & Nettles, M. T. (1990). Minority student access to, and persistence and performance in, college: A review of trends and research literature. In J. C. Smart (Ed.), *Higher Education: Handbook of Theory and Research*, 6, 35–105. New York: Agathon Press.

Murguia, E., Padilla, R., & Pavel, M. (1991). Ethnicity and the concept of social integration in Tinto's model of institutional departure. *Journal of College Student Development*, 32, 433–439.

Nelis, (1989, February 6). *Syracuse Post Standard* (daily), Syracuse, NY.

Nettles, M. T. (1985). *The causes and consequences of college students' performance: A focus on Black and White students' attrition rates, progression rates and grade point averages.* Nashville: Tennessee Higher Education Commission.

Nettles, M. T., Ed. (1988). *Toward Black undergraduate student equality in American higher education.* New York: Greenwood.

Nettles, M. T. (1991). *Assessing progress in minority access and achievement in American higher education* (ECS Working Papers No. PA-91-1). Colorado: Education Commission of the States.

Nettles, M. T., & Johnson, J. R. (1987). Race, sex, and other factors as determinants of college students' socialization. *Journal of College Student Personnel*, 28(6), 512–24.

Ogbu, J. U. (1978). *Minority education and caste: The American system in cross-cultural perspective.* New York: Academic Press.

Ogbu, J. U. (1981). Schooling in the ghetto an ecological perspective on community & home influences. Conference paper prepared for NIE Conference on Follow Through, Philadelphia, February 10th & 11th, 1981

Pascarella, E. T., & Terenzini, P. T. (1983). Predicting voluntary freshman year persistence/withdrawal behavior in a residential university: A path analytical validation of Tinto's model. *Journal of Educational Psychology*, (75) 215–226.

Pascarella, E., & Terenzini, P. (1991). *How college affects students*. San Francisco: Jossey-Bass

Perry, W. G., Jr. (1970). *Forms of intellectual and ethical development in the college years: A scheme*. New York: Holt, Rinehart and Winston, Inc.

Perry, W. G., Jr. (1981). Cognitive and ethical growth. In A. Chickering et al. (Eds.). *The modern American college: Responding to the new realities of diverse students and a changing society*. San Francisco: Jossey-Bass.

Pinderhughes, E. (1989). *Understanding race and ethnicity and power: The key to efficacy in clinical practice*. New York: The Free Press.

Racism 101. (1988). Transcript. Frontline #612: Boston: WGBH Educational Foundation.

Richardson, R. C., Jr., & Bender L. W. (1985). *Students in urban settings: Achieving the baccalaureate degree*. Washington DC: American Association for Higher Education.

Schaefer, R. T. (1993). *Racial and ethnic groups*. (5th ed.). New York: Harper Collins College Publishers.

Shea. C. (1995, April 28). Under UCLA's elaborate system race makes a big difference. *The Chronicle of Higher Education*, p. A12.

Smith, A. W. (1991). Personal traits, institutional prestige, racial attitudes, and Black student academic performance in college. In W. R. Allen, et al. (Eds.). *College in Black and White: African American students in predominantly White and in historically Black public universities*. Albany: State University of New York Press. (pp. 111–126).

Smith, H. H. (1991). The impact of supportive services on performance of disadvantaged students attending a predominantly White university. (Doctoral dissertation, Cornell University, 1991). *Dissertation Abstracts International.*

Spencer, M. B., Brookins, G. K., & Allen, W. R. (Eds.). (1985). *Beginnings: The social and affective development of Black children.* Hillsdale, NJ: Lawrence Erlbaum Associates, Publishers.

Steele, C. M. (1992, April). Race and the Schooling of Black Americans. *The Atlantic Monthly,* 69(4), 68–78.

Stikes, C. S. (1984). *Black students in higher education.* Carbondale: Southern Illinois University Press.

Syracuse Chamber of Commerce, 572 South Salina Street, Syracuse, New York, 13202. Annual Report. 1993

Syracuse University *FACTS.* (1987–1988, 1988–1989, 1992–1993, 1994–1995), Publications Office, Syracuse University, Syracuse, New York, 13244.

Syracuse University, (1991–1992). *Syracuse University Student Handbook.* Publications Office, Syracuse University, Syracuse, New York, 13244.

Thomas, G. E. (1984). *Black college students and factors influencing their major field choice.* Atlanta: Southern Education Foundation.

Tinto, V. (1975). Dropouts from education: A Theoretical Synthesis of recent research. *Educational Research,* 45: 89-125

Tinto, V. (1986). Theories of student departure revisited. In John C. Smart (ed.) *Higher education: Handbook of theory and research.* Agathon Press. (pp. 359–384).

Tinto, V. (1987). *Leaving college: Rethinking the causes and cures of student attrition.* Chicago: University of Chicago Press

Tinto, V. (1994). *Leaving College: Rethinking the causes and cures of Student Attrition.* 2nd ed. Chicago: University of Chicago Press

Weidman, J. (1989). Undergraduate socialization: A conceptual approach. In J. Smart (Ed.). *Higher education: handbook of theory and practice.* New York: Agathon Press. pp. 289–315.

West, C. (1993). *Race matters.* Boston: Beacon Press.

Williams, A. (1995). "A Perception" in R. Deborah Davis. African American students' perspectives of their experiences at a predominantly White institution: A qualitative piece of the retention puzzle. Syracuse University, 1996. *Dissertation Abstracts International*.

Willie, C. V. (1981). *The ivory and ebony towers.* Lexington: Lexington Books, D. C. Heath and Co.

Willie, C. V., Garibaldi, A. M., & Reed, W. L. (Eds). (1991). *The Education of African-Americans.* Westport: Auburn House.

Willie, C. V., & McCord, A. (Eds.). (1972) *Black students at White colleges.* New York: Praeger.

Yonai, B. A. (1991). The Effects of a Pre-freshman Summer Bridge Program on Student Persistence into the Sophomore Year. (Doctoral Dissertation. Syracuse University, 1991). *Dissertation Abstracts International*.

Zack, N. (1993). *Race and mixed race.* Philadelphia: Temple University Press.

✤ Index

A

a sense of competence, 115
AAS, 17. See African American Studies Department
academic advisement, 133
academic and social integration, 22
academic environment, 3
academic issues, 69
academic schedule, 56
academic studies, 6
acceptable
    not acceptable, 85
accepted, 9
    good enough, 65
    to be accepted, 64
    to be or not to be, 68
achieving at a lower rate, 1
Adler & Adler, 7, 22
adolescence to adulthood developmental changes", 37
affirm one's Blackness, 117
African American
    females, 69
African American Studies (AAS), 116
African descent, 45
African diaspora, 4
Ajzen & Fishbein,, 21
Alexander Astin, 5. See Astin
Allen, 2, 7, 21, 47, 137, 139, 140, 143, 144
Allen et al, 22, 47
Altbach & Lomotey, 22, 111
American Council on Education, 19
anticipatory socialization, 32, 40, 136
Armstrong-West & de la Teja, 1
Asante & Noor Al-Deen, 21
assimilation, 110
assumptions, 3, 26, 34
    tenets, 29
    tenets of campus atmosphere, 3
Astin, 2, 5, 21, 22, 138
attrition, 21
autonomy stage, 42
Avatus Stone, 8

B

Bean, 5 *See* John Bean
Bean, John P,. 21
being suspect, 134
Being Visible and Invisible, 87
belonging, 60
    a certain level of comfort, 53
    a place to breathe, 69
    feeling like you belong, 76
    safe haven, 69
benefit of social support, 15
Bentler & Speckart, 21
Bing '66, Dave, 9
Biracial, 2, 4, 17, 51, 79, 82, 83, 136
Black and Hispanic, 26
    weekend, 48, 49
Black and Latino, 7
Black athletes, 22
Black children, 21, 114, 144
Black community, 13
Black experience, 2, 18
    an integrated high school, 22
    fifth through seventh semesters, 23
    incompatibility of expectations, 76
    negative and positive, 3
    over a five year period, 2
    with Engineering, 94
Black faculty, 111
Black feminism, 93
Black identity, 23, 39, 43, 45, 113, 117
Black Issues in Higher Education, 135
Black organizations, 84
Black role models, 16
Black student enrollment, 13
Black Student Experience, 29
Black students, 1
    activism, 48
    anxiety, 66
    cultural backgrounds, 7
    designated by color. *See* capitalizatized terms
    disparity in treatment, 1
    disproportionately recruited, 9
    family encouragement, 21
    from the cities, 135

Index

GPA and test scores, 22
graduating from, 3
how they were perceived, 27
identified in racial terms. See capitalized terms
in contrast, 77
initial concerns, 47
initial contacts, 56
life decisions, 23
percentage of growth, 3
perception, 65
perspective on housing, 52
sense of competence, 41
sports, 50
statistics, 20
typical, 68
viewed as learners, 24
Black undergraduates, 7. See Black students
Black/African American. See Black students
Blacks in College, 47
Blackwell, 21
Bogdan and Biklen, 25, 47
Boule Journal, 9
Brown '57, Jim , 8
Brown '61, John, 8
Bryant '29, Gladys, 8

C

Cabrera, 32, 47
campus hierarchy, 58
CAMPUS INCONGRUITY, 44
Campus Visits, 48
    initial impressions, 48
capitalized
    Black, White, Biracial, 2. See Black students
career-planning strategies, 23
Caribbean Americans, 17
Carter & Wilson, 19
Change
    a definition, 33
Chestang, Leon W., 18
Chickering, 23, 30
Chickering & Reisser, 38, 112
Chickering's seven vectors, 34
Chronicle of Higher Education,, 19
Civil Rights legislation, 9
Civil Rights Movement, 21, 75
Classroom Experience, 90
cognitive growth, 47

Cohen '57, Vincent, 8
College impact theories, 30
Colleges in Black and White, 7
common experiences, 79
Common Themes, 134
complexity, 34, 55
Complexity of the College Experience, 40
connotations of terms, 5
constituents, 15
Cope & Hanna, 2, 22
coping with problems, 33
Cross, 23, 30. *See* William Cross
Cross, William, 39, 42
cultural distinctions, 45
culturally, 11
culture, 63
    different, 123
culture shock, 85

D

daily assaults, 83
Daily Orange, 16, 17, 18, 126, 139
    student newspaper, 6
Davis, 1, 15, 46, 47, 54, 92, 106, 114, 139, 145
Deskins, 7, 19, 20
development
    a definition, 34
developmental, 33
    changes, 37
    models, 33
    theories, 34
Devereau '56-'57, John, 8
diaspora, 25
differences, 116, 122
disadvantage, 68
    economically, 68, 134
    educationally, 68
disciplinary probation, 18
disharmony, 18
disproportionately recruited, 9
diversity, 18, 76, 126
DIVERSITY INQUIRY, 44
Division of Student Support and Development, 24
Division of Supportive Services, 28
dominant social group, 74
dropout rates, 121
DuBois, W. E. B,. 9

E

economic deprivation, 24
Encounter, 39
　stage, 41
encounter stage, 116
enrollment, 19, 20, 27
epigenetic principle, 30
Erikson, 29, 115, 118
Erikson, Erik, 115
ESTABLISHING IDENTITY, 44
ethnic construct, 33
ethnic definition, 7
ethnicity, 33, 73
European American, 4
European Americans, 132
expectations, 68

F

faculty perception, 45
family and community, 51
family support
　financial aid, 68
　groomed by their families, 66
　independence, 95
　support of his father, 65
first-generation college students, 37
Fleming, 2, 15, 21, 23, 47, 128, 140
Fleming, Jacqueline, 47, 76
fly in the buttermilk syndrome, 107
Fordham & Ogbu, 21, 23, 43
fraternities, 14, 79
from the city, 134

G

Gibbs, 5, 21, 77, 140
Gibbs, Jewel T. *See* Gibbs
Gibson & Ogbu, 5, 22
Goal Assessment, 117
GOAL CLARIFICATION, 44, 118
grades, 69
graduation figures, 20
Graduation rates, 74
Graduation Rates, 134
Greek letter organizations, 14
growth and development, 29
Gruin & Epps, 21

H

Hasbrouck, Ellsworth, 8
Hare, 17
HBCU, 7, 74, 76
Helms & Parham, 23, 45
Helms, Janet, 42
HEOP, 24, 57, 113, 134
　compensatory education, 24
heterogeneous group, 25
Hollins, 42
hostile, 122
hostile environment, 2, 18, 25, 139
How College Affects Students, 33
Hunter '65, Billy, 9
hurtful interactions, 71

I

identity, 23, 42, 82
IDENTITY CONFUSION, 44, 116
Immersion / Emersion, 39
in the spotlight, 60
incongruity, 115
inconsistency of treatment, 18
incorporation, 31
independent colleges, 10. *See*
　predominantly White campus
individual self-concept. *See* identity
injustice, 18
institutional departure, 30
institutional fit, 22
　theory, 22
institutional racism, 109, 111
institutionalized racism, 60, 136
institutions as socializing organizations, 33
integration, 38
interactionist theories, 31
interactions with faculty, 67
interactions with the financial aid
　processes., 122
Internalization, 39
Internalization Commitment, 39
interpersonal interactions, 109
interpersonal relationships, 35
interracial education, 118
intimidation and apprehension, 107
Irvine, 21, 30, 42, 74, 126, 141

Index

J
just BEING, 84

K
key factors, 9
King, 42

L
Lang & Ford, 22
Leaving College, 31
Lewis,, 9
Little '67, Floyd, 9
Lynn '32, Conrad, 8

M
Mackey '63, John, 9
male students, 123
Merton, 40, 114, 136. *See* anticipatory socialization
microcosm, 19
minorities, 19
Minorities in Higher Education, 21
Minorities on Campus, 12
minority faculty, 16
Minority Receptions, 49
Morris, Horace, 8
Morrison, 19, 49
Morrison, Toni, 119
Mow & Nettles, 2, 5, 7, 22
multicultural living, 134
multiplicity, 42
multiplistic
    frame of reference, 36
    position, 36
    way of thinking, 42
Murguia, et al., 32, 33

N
National Association of Negro Business and Professional Women's Clubs (NANBPWC), 15
National Society of Black Engineers (NSBE), 15, 95
Negro race, 9
Nettles, 5, 23, 47
Nettles & Johnson, 23
Nettles, et al, 2, 21
Nettles, Michael, 5
Nigresence, 39
nonacademic events, 26

O
Office of Multicultural Affairs, 14, 87
Ogbu, 21, 126, 140, 142, 143
Organizational theories, 31
other minorities, 4

P
Parham, Thomas, 42
Pascarella & Terenzini, 2, 23, 30, 32, 47
Pascarella and Terrenzini, 22
passing for White", 5
People of color, 4
perception, 59, 70
    institutional, 134
    stereotypical, 71
Perception
    different, 113
perdominantly White
    educational system, 6
Perry, 23, 30, 36, 40
    Multiplistic frame of reference, 36
persistence, 21
persisters, 23, 129
personal problems, 23
perspective, 61, 80
    a Black, 30, 57
    cultural, 44
    differing, 59, 79
    students', 106
pilot study, 27
Pinderhughes, 78, 110
Pinderhughes, Elaine, 78
power brokers, 132
Precollege
    activities, 49
    transition, 27
predominantly white, 40, 137
predominantly White
    campus, 9, 25, 84, 115, 119
    environment, 106
    institution, 7, 13, 76, 121
    sororities and fraternities, 124
    university, 51, 78, 95, 109, 118, 130

Predominantly White
    institution, 113
Preencounter, 39
    stage, 40
preencounter stage, 113
pre-freshman program. See Summer
    Institute
preorientation, 48, 49
pre-professional program, 49
proportion of Blacks, 11
proximity
    to New York City, 3
psychosocial theories, 30

Q

quality of life, 21

R

Race, 29, 61, 73
    a biological term, 78
Racial incidents, 18
racism, 74, 75, 79, 81, 84, 85, 91, 110, 117
racist, 122
recruitment, 76
    and enrollment, 10
    and retention, 19, 76
    and support, 109
    programs, 73
    purpose of, 3
    retention, 68
    successful, 19
    trends, 10
reference group, 136
Relativism stage, 44
residence life, 52
retention, 21
Retreat, 36
Richardson & Bender, 21
role models, 16
roommate, 51 52, 56, 123
    Black, 53

S

S.A.S., 15, 17, 48
SAT scores, 68
Schine Student Center, 13, 27
School of Engineering, 123, 131
segregated, 123
self-fulfilling prophesy, 19
sense of competence, 41
separation, 31
separatism, 17, 53
Seven Vectors, 34
Shades of Black, 43
Shadows of the Black College Student
    Experience, 41
SI, 24, 28, 55
    privileges of, 57
    students, 55
SI students, 58
Sidat-Singh, Wilmeth, 8
skin color, 7. *See* black students
Smith, A. W., 112
Smith, H. H. 5
Smith, H. 24
social climate, 3, 60
social injustice, 18
social integration, 6, 23
social interaction, 27, 32
    Black/White, 78
    concept of, 33
    understanding the norms of, 125
socialization, 22, 23, 43
socioemotional support, 54
sororities, 14, 79, 82
south campus housing, 52
Spencer, 21
Spencer et al, 23
sponsored programs, 69
Steele, 42
stereotype, 67
    because of, 33
    Black and poor, 121
    held by, 79
    notions of behavior, 32
    of Black male, 106
    of New York City Black students, 135
    originating, 1
    promulgated by science, 5
    stereotypical, 64
stigma, 71
Stikes, 21
stopping out, 37
stress, 133
Student African American Society (S.A.S.),
    15
student departure, 21, 31
student empowerment, 24
student persistence. *See* persistence
student retention, 5
students' perceptions of their experiences, 5.
    See Black experiences

Summer Institute, 6, 24, 27, 51, 121
    interpersonal skills, 55
    people, 55
    stigmatizing, 58
    student benefits, 54
Supportive services programs, 69
Syracuse Herald American, 8
Syracuse Herald-Journal, 13
Syracuse University, 3, 4, 6, 7, 8, 9, 10, 11, 13, 14, 15, 16, 19, 24, 26, 48, 50, 51, 70

T

Temporizing, 36
term. *See* capitalized terms
terms
    foreign, minority, and majority, 17
the City, 56, 81,
    from the city, 59
The Lubin House, 19, 49
    experience, 19
the only Black, 62
    the only, 60
    the only one, 61
The Post Standard, 111
The Racial Crisis in American Higher Education, 111
The Record, 18
theory of nigrescence, 34
Thomas, 21, 141, 144
Tinto, 5, 22, 135, 30
Tinto model, 21, 28, 30, 33
Tinto, Vincent,. *See* Tinto

transition, 31

V

Validate Identity, 117
Van Gennep, 31

W

Weidman, 23, 32, 40, 114
Weidman, John, *See* Weidman
    four-stage socialization process, 32
what it's like to be a minority, 115
where the student lived, 23
Wille & McCord, 21
Williams, Angela, 46
Williams, Everett Browning, 8
Williams '50, John, 8
Willie & McCord, 7, 21
Willie et al, 22
Willie, 21

Y

Yonai, 24, 27, 112

Z

Zack, 73

Studies in the Postmodern Theory of Education

General Editors
Joe L. Kincheloe & Shirley R. Steinberg

Counterpoints publishes the most compelling and imaginative books being written in education today. Grounded on the theoretical advances in criticism, feminism, and postmodernism in the last two decades of the twentieth century, Counterpoints engages the meaning of these innovations in various forms of educational expression. Committed to the proposition that theoretical literature should be accessible to a variety of audiences, the series insists that its authors avoid esoteric and jargonistic languages that transform educational scholarship into an elite discourse for the initiated. Scholarly work matters only to the degree it affects consciousness and practice at multiple sites. Counterpoints' editorial policy is based on these principles and the ability of scholars to break new ground, to open new conversations, to go where educators have never gone before.

For additional information about this series or for the submission of manuscripts, please contact:
        Joe L. Kincheloe & Shirley R. Steinberg
        c/o Peter Lang Publishing, Inc.
        275 Seventh Avenue, 28th floor
        New York, New York 10001

To order other books in this series, please contact our Customer Service Department:
        (800) 770-LANG (within the U.S.)
        (212) 647-7706 (outside the U.S.)
        (212) 647-7707 FAX

Or browse online by series:
        www.peterlangusa.com